outcome
mapping

Outcome Mapping

Building Learning and Reflection
into Development Programs

*Sarah Earl, Fred Carden,
and Terry Smutylo*

Foreword by Michael Quinn Patton

INTERNATIONAL DEVELOPMENT RESEARCH CENTRE
Ottawa ▪ Cairo ▪ Dakar ▪ Montevideo ▪ Nairobi ▪ New Delhi ▪ Singapore

© **International Development Research Centre 2001**

Published by the International Development Research Centre
PO Box 8500, Ottawa, ON, Canada K1G 3H9
http://www.idrc.ca

National Library of Canada cataloguing in publication data

Earl, Sarah, 1971–

Outcome mapping : building learning and reflection into development
programs

Includes bibliographical references.
ISBN 0-88936-959-3

1. Economic development projects — Evaluation.
2. Technical assistance — Developing countries — Evaluation.
3. International cooperation.
I. Carden, Fred.
II. Smutylo, Terry.
III. International Development Research Centre (Canada)
IV. Title.

HD75.9E72 2001   338.91   C2001-980277-3

IDRC Books endeavours to produce environmentally friendly publications. All paper used is recycled as well as recyclable. All inks and coatings are vegetable-based products. The full catalogue of IDRC Books is available at http://www.idrc.ca/booktique/.

CONTENTS

FOREWORD

Imagine a map ... drawn from your memory instead of from the atlas. It is made of strong places stitched together by the vivid threads of transforming journeys. It contains all the things you learned from the land and shows where you learned them .... Think of this map as a living thing, not a chart but a tissue of stories that grows half-consciously with each experience. It tells where and who you are with respect to the earth, and in times of stress or disorientation it gives you the bearings you need in order to move on. We all carry such maps within us as sentient and reflective beings, and we depend upon them unthinkingly, as we do upon language or thought .... And it is part of wisdom, to consider this ecological aspect of our identity.

– John Tallmadge, *Meeting the Tree of Life* (1997: IX)

Maps are cognitive guides. They locate us, helping us to figure out where we are now in relation to where we've been, and to plan where we're going. It is altogether appropriate, then, that IDRC's Evaluation Unit has chosen the metaphor of mapping to guide those interested in development on the sometimes confusing, even frightening journey through the hazardous territory of outcomes.

The language can be daunting: outcomes, impacts, goals, objectives, purposes, mission, and outputs — and these terms just scratch the surface. The questions can overwhelm. What's the difference between evaluation and monitoring? How do short-term changes relate to intermediate changes and long-term results? What kinds of results count as outcomes? How can the need for accountability be balanced against the need for learning? Then there's the attribution problem. To what extent and in what ways can one establish a causal linkage between activities, outputs, outcomes, and impacts? Who gets credit for results? What kinds of evidence are credible? What's the unit of analysis? What role does stakeholder involvement play in all this?

The territory of developmental change and evaluation is vast, complex, and ever-changing. Trying to manoeuver through that territory one is likely to encounter deep ravines of uncertainty, mountains of data, and side-tracks that lead nowhere. It sure would help to have a map to the territory. This manual on outcome mapping can't provide the specific map you need for your own territory, for each territory is unique and presents its own challenges, but this manual will tell you **how to create your own map**. It will guide you through the language forest of terminology. It will show you how to navigate the winding river of a results chain. It will help you figure out where the boundaries are of the territory you are exploring and provide assistance in identifying "boundary partners" to accompany you on the outcomes journey. It will show you how to construct a strategy map and figure out progress markers.

A vision of useful and meaningful evaluation — evaluation in support of learning — undergirds this manual and is essential to understanding its important contributions. A sophisticated understanding of contemporary evaluation issues informs what may appear as simple mapping exercises provided here. One of the strengths of the manual is that it cuts through the complex evaluation literature, extracting deceptively straightforward and commonsensical wisdom from the many divisions and debates within the evaluation community based on a deep knowledge of, and explicit value premises related to, development. The staff of IDRC's Evaluation Unit have long been working to support **learning** as a primary outcome of development program evaluation. They have observed that longer term outcomes and impacts often occur a long way downstream from program implementation and may not take the form anticipated. These longer term outcomes depend on responsiveness to context-specific factors, creating diversity across initiatives. The outcomes examined include the depth and breadth of involvement by many stakeholders, processes that become results in and of themselves when done in ways that are sustainable. These characteristics make it difficult for external agencies to identify and attribute specific outcomes to specific components of their programs or to aggregate and compare results across initiatives.

Outcome Mapping offers a methodology that can be used to create planning, monitoring, and evaluation mechanisms enabling organizations to document, learn from, and report on their achievements. It is designed to assist in understanding an organization's results, while recognizing that contributions by other actors are essential to achieving the kinds of sustainable, large-scale improvements in human and ecological well-being toward which the organization is working. The innovations introduced in *Outcome Mapping* provide ways of overcoming some of the barriers to learning faced by evaluators and development partners. Attribution and measuring downstream results are dealt with through a more direct focus on transformations in the actions of the main actors. The methodology has also shown promise for across-portfolio learning in that it facilitates standardization of indicators without losing the richness in each case's story, thus combining quantitative and qualitative approaches.

An old hiking adage warns that "the map is not the territory." True enough. You need to keep your eyes open and watch for unexpected outcroppings and changes in the terrain. But without a map, you can get so lost in the territory that it's hard to even figure out where you started much less find your way to an outcome. *Outcome Mapping* provides not only a guide to essential evaluation map-making, but also a guide to learning and increased effectiveness, and affirmation that being attentive along the journey is as important as, and critical to, arriving at a destination.

Michael Quinn Patton
17 September 2001

Michael Quinn Patton is an independent organizational development and evaluation consultant. He is the author of five books on program evaluation including a new edition of *Utilization-Focused Evaluation: The New Century Text* (1997). The two previous editions of that book have been used in over 300 universities around the world. His other books are *Qualitative Evaluation and Research Methods* (1990, 2nd edition); *Creative Evaluation* (1987); *Practical Evaluation* (1982); and *Culture and Evaluation* (1985). Patton is former President of the American Evaluation Association. He is the only recipient of both the Alva and Gunner Myrdal Award from the Evaluation Research Society for "outstanding contributions to evaluation use and practice" and the Paul F. Lazarsfeld Award for lifetime contributions to evaluation theory from the American Evaluation Association. He has a vast academic background and is a faculty member of the Union Institute Graduate School, which specializes in individually designed, nonresidential, nontraditional, and interdisciplinary doctoral programs. He also has been involved with the development of the African Evaluation Association.

PREFACE

The International Development Research Centre's (IDRC) conceptual and practical work over the past few years with donors, Southern research institutions, program staff, and evaluation experts has brought to the fore a fundamental problem with existing approaches to reporting on development impacts. When referring to "impact," development organizations usually mean significant and lasting changes in the well-being of large numbers of intended beneficiaries. These changes are the results for which donors expect accountability. This is problematic because the complexity and fluidity of development processes mean that achieving such impacts requires the involvement of a variety of actors, often over a considerable period of time. When large-scale change — or impact — manifests itself, it is often the product of a confluence of events over which no single agency has control or can realistically claim full credit.

In response to this problem, several of IDRC's programs and its Evaluation Unit have been working with Dr Barry Kibel, of the Pacific Institute for Research and Evaluation, to adapt his Outcome Engineering approach to the development research context. Outcome Engineering was developed to help Dr Kibel's clients in the American social service sector meet their reporting needs while improving their performance. Although individuals being treated by social service providers in the United States face different constraints and require different types of support than international applied research institutions, the conceptual and practical problems associated with assessing results have proven to be quite similar. Some of the main adaptations have related to modifying the basic unit of analysis from the individual to groups, organizations, consortia, and networks. Adapting the methodology has been greatly enhanced through methodological collaboration with the West African Rural Foundation (Senegal) and testing with the Nagaland Empowerment of People Through Economic Development Project (India) and the International Model Forest Network Secretariat (Canada). The result is a methodology, called "Outcome Mapping," that characterizes and assesses the contributions made by development projects, programs, or organizations to the achievement of outcomes. This methodology is applicable during the design stage or during a midterm or ex-post assessment.

This manual is intended as an introduction to the theory and concepts of Outcome Mapping and as a guide to conducting an Outcome Mapping workshop. Although Outcome Mapping may be appropriate in various contexts, it has primarily been tested by development research organizations and programs working in Canada, Africa, Latin America, and Asia. This manual reflects that perspective and Outcome Mapping may have to be adapted to be used with groups other than our constituency of researchers, scientific organizations, government officials, policymakers, and NGOs (for example, communities).

Outcome Mapping has been developed in organizations where monitoring and evaluation are primarily intended to help with program learning and improvement. The tenor of a program's approach to Outcome Mapping will necessarily be influenced by its own and its donor's perspectives on monitoring and evaluation. Outcome Mapping will only be as empowering, participatory, and learning-oriented as the program that implements it. Outcome Mapping takes into consideration the threats and anxiety that can be associated with planning, monitoring and evaluation, especially in a donor/recipient relationship. It offers a participatory methodology that can help programs develop a system that can meet both accountability and learning needs.

Section 1 presents the theory underpinning Outcome Mapping — its purpose and uses, as well as how it differs from other approaches to monitoring and evaluation in the development field, such as logic models. Section 2 presents an overview of the workshop approach to Outcome Mapping — including the steps of the workshop, as well as how to select participants and facilitators. Sections 3, 4, and 5 outline each of the stages of an Outcome Mapping workshop, suggest a process that can be followed by the facilitator, and provide examples of the finished "products."

Outcome Mapping is a dynamic methodology that is currently being tested at the project, program, and organizational levels. Its conceptual development has been a collaborative effort between IDRC's Evaluation Unit, program initiatives, secretariats, and partner organizations. We would especially like to thank a number of organizations who have been instrumental in field testing the approach: the Sustainable Use of Biodiversity (team leader, Wardie Leppan) and the Alternative Approaches to Natural Resource Management (team leader, Simon Carter) program initiatives of IDRC, Fadel Diamé and the staff of the

West African Rural Foundation, K. Kevichusa and the staff of the Nagaland Empowerment of People Through Economic Development Project team, Sonia Salas and the Condesan Arracacha project, Jim Armstrong and the Governance Network, and Fred Johnson and the International Model Forest Network Secretariat staff. For their valuable comments on the content and structure of this manual, we thank Marie-Hélène Adrien, Charles Lusthaus, Fiona Mackenzie, Nancy MacPherson, Greg Mason, John Mayne, Alex Moiseev, Carroll Salomon, and Ian Smillie. Outcome Mapping remains a work in progress, and so we look forward to receiving your comments and suggestions toward its improvement. You can reach us at the address noted below. Your comments will be valued and will enrich our work.

Evaluation Unit
International Development Research Centre
PO Box 8500
Ottawa, Ontario
Canada K1G 3H9

Phone: (+1 613) 236-6163 (ext. 2350)
Fax: (+1 613) 563-0815
E-mail: evaluation@idrc.ca

You can learn more about the Evaluation Unit's work with Outcome Mapping on our Web site at www.idrc.ca/evaluation.

Sarah Earl
Fred Carden
Terry Smutylo

1 OUTCOME MAPPING: THE THEORY

What is Outcome Mapping?

Outcome Mapping focuses on one specific type of result: outcomes as behavioural change. **Outcomes are defined as changes in the behaviour, relationships, activities, or actions of the people, groups, and organizations with whom a program works directly.** These outcomes can be logically linked to a program's activities, although they are not necessarily directly caused by them. These changes are aimed at contributing to specific aspects of human and ecological well-being by providing partners with new tools, techniques, and resources to contribute to the development process. **Boundary partners are those individuals, groups, and organizations with whom the program interacts directly and with whom the program anticipates opportunities for influence.** Most activities will involve multiple outcomes because they have multiple boundary partners. By using Outcome Mapping, a program is not claiming the achievement of development impacts; rather, the focus is on its contributions to outcomes. These outcomes, in turn, enhance the possibility of development impacts — but the relationship is not necessarily a direct one of cause and effect. Ultimately, all organizations engaged in international development want their work to contribute to long-term development impacts. However, this is rarely accomplished by the work of a single actor (especially an external donor agency). The complexity of the development process makes it extremely difficult to assess impact (especially for an external donor agency seeking attribution). Furthermore, focusing assessment on long-term development impacts does not necessarily provide the kind of information and feedback that programs require to improve their performance. For these reasons, Outcome Mapping focuses on outcomes instead of impact, while recognizing the importance of impact as the ultimate goal toward which programs work.

Outcome Mapping assumes that the boundary partners control change and that, as external agents, development programs only facilitate the process by providing access to new resources, ideas, or opportunities for a certain period of time. A focus on the behaviour of the boundary partners does not mean that the program decides how, when, and why those partners will change. In fact, by focusing on changes in behaviour, Outcome Mapping makes explicit something that has been accepted by development practitioners for a long time: the most successful programs are those that devolve power and responsibility to endogenous actors.

As development is essentially about people relating to each other and their environments, the focus of Outcome Mapping is on people. The originality of the methodology is its shift away from assessing the development impact of a program (defined as changes in state — for example, policy relevance, poverty alleviation, or reduced conflict) and toward changes in the behaviours, relationships, actions or activities of the people, groups, and organizations with whom a development program works directly. This shift significantly alters the way a program understands its goals and assesses its performance and results. Outcome Mapping establishes a vision of the human, social, and environmental betterment to which the program hopes to contribute and then focuses monitoring and evaluation on factors and actors within that program's direct sphere of influence. The program's contributions to development are planned and assessed based on its influence on the partners with whom it is working to effect change. At its essence, development is accomplished by, and for, people. Therefore, this is the central concept of Outcome Mapping.

Outcome Mapping does not belittle the importance of changes in state (such as cleaner water or a stronger economy) but instead argues that for each change in state there are correlating changes in behaviour. Many programs can better plan for and assess their contributions to development by focusing on behaviour. This is particularly true for programs that focus on capacity building. For example, a program's objective may be to provide communities with access to cleaner water by installing purification filters. Traditionally, the method of evaluating the results of this program would be to count the number of filters installed and measure changes in the level of contaminants in the water before and after the filters were installed. A focus on changes in behaviour begins instead from the premise that water does not remain clean without people being able to maintain its quality over time. The program's outcomes are therefore evaluated in terms of whether those responsible for water purity in the communities not only have, but use, the appropriate tools, skills, and knowledge to monitor the contaminant levels, change filters, or bring in experts when required. Outcome Mapping provides a method for development programs to plan for and assess the capacities that they are helping to build in the people, groups, and organizations who will ultimately be responsible for improving the well-being of their communities. Outcome Mapping does not attempt to replace the more traditional forms of evaluation, which focus on changes in conditions or in the state of well-being. Instead, Outcome Mapping supplements other forms of evaluation by focusing specifically on related behavioural change.

Three Stages of Outcome Mapping

Outcome Mapping is divided into three stages. The first stage, Intentional Design, helps a program establish consensus on the macro level changes it will help to bring about and plan the strategies it will use. It helps answer four questions: **Why?** (What is the vision to which the program wants to contribute?); **Who?** (Who are the program's boundary partners?); **What?** (What are the changes that are being sought?); and **How?** (How will the program contribute to the change process?). The second stage, Outcome and Performance Monitoring, provides a framework for the ongoing monitoring of the program's actions and the boundary partners' progress toward the achievement of outcomes. It is based largely on systematized self-assessment. It provides the following data collection tools for elements identified in the Intentional Design stage: an "Outcome Journal" (progress markers); a "Strategy Journal" (strategy maps); and a "Performance Journal" (organizational practices). The third stage, Evaluation Planning, helps the program identify evaluation priorities and develop an evaluation plan. Figure 1 (next page) illustrates the three stages of Outcome Mapping.

Figure 1. Three Stages of Outcome Mapping

The process for identifying the macro-level changes and designing the monitoring framework and evaluation plan is intended to be participatory and, wherever feasible, can involve the full range of stakeholders, including boundary partners. Outcome Mapping is based on principles of participation and purposefully includes those implementing the program in the design and data collection so as to encourage ownership and use of findings. It is intended to be used as a consciousness-raising, consensus-building, and empowerment tool for those working directly in the development program.

Outcome Mapping introduces monitoring and evaluation considerations at the planning stage of a program. It also unites process and outcome evaluation by collecting data on the program's success in implementing its strategies and the results being achieved by its boundary partners. Separating process and outcome evaluation is misleading, because it implies that an organization achieves outcomes as a direct result of implementing a program. But obtaining results in international development is not that straightforward. Focusing monitoring and evaluation on the program's boundary partners makes it possible to obtain useful feedback about the program's performance and results within its sphere of influence. The logic underpinning this is that the resources for monitoring and evaluation are limited and are best spent on studies that will allow for better understanding of the influences of a program's work, so as to improve its performance. Also, having a system in place that regularly collects credible data on external results and internal performance can help a program meet its accountability requirements to its donor or management.

Rather than attempting a "rolling-up" of evaluation information from a number of disparate activities, Outcome Mapping provides a method for a program to set overall intentions and strategies, monitor its contributions to outcomes, and target priority areas for detailed evaluation studies. As a whole, Outcome Mapping provides a program with a continuous system for thinking holistically and strategically about how it intends to achieve results. It also provides the tools for a program to tell its performance story. It does so by monitoring in three key areas: changes in the behaviour of partners; the program's strategies; and the way in which it functions as an organizational unit. By actively engaging the team in the monitoring and evaluation process, Outcome Mapping empowers them to articulate, with accurate and reliable data, both what they do to support outcomes and the depth of change in their partners. In essence, it tries to implant the passion and enthusiasm of programming into the assessment process. Outcome Mapping moves away from the notion that monitoring and evaluation are done to a program, and, instead, actively engages the team in the design of a monitoring framework and evaluation plan and promotes self-assessment.

Why Not Impact?

As they are currently applied, the concepts of "attribution" and "impact" can limit the potential of programs to learn from evaluations of development efforts. In light of shrinking international development aid dollars and the need to optimize what is left, donors are increasingly basing funding decisions on their recipients' abilities to demonstrate "impact." In development terms, this typically means providing evidence that a particular program has brought about a sustainable improvement in the environment or in the well-being of a large number of targeted beneficiaries. Methodologically, this requires isolating the key factors that caused the desired results and attributing them to a particular agency or set of activities.

For development agencies, this means identifying and measuring the net, positive effects as they result directly from the activities that those agencies support. In the literature, there are few good examples where this has been done. IDRC has long struggled with this challenge in relation to development research — a struggle made more difficult by IDRC's style of program delivery. Research results improve peoples' lives via long, busy, discontinuous pathways. Tracing the connections is at best unreliable and at worst impossible. This disconnect between important upstream contributions and downstream goals has been recognized in evaluation circles for a long time. In his 1967 book, *Evaluative Research*, Edward A. Suchman stated (p. 55.):

> *The extent to which immediate and intermediate goals can be divorced from ultimate goals as valid in themselves poses a difficult question. Certainly there is a tremendous amount of activity, perhaps the largest portion of all public service work, devoted to the successful attainment of immediate and intermediate goals which appear to have only a very indirect bearing upon ultimate goals.*

While the push to measure, demonstrate, and be accountable for development impact is most obvious within the donor community, it has also made its way into recipient agencies and communities through requirements such as "logical framework analysis" (LFA) or "results-based management" (RBM) for planning and reporting on activities to donors. Consequently, the search for impact has become an accepted and dominant part of the development discourse. Nonetheless when donors and recipients try to be accountable for achieving impact, they are severely limiting their potential for understanding how and why impact occurs. The drive to claim credit interferes with the creation of knowledge. As one colleague has expressed it, the singular focus on results yields "clueless feedback."

There are a number of ways in which the practices of donor agencies relating to impact contradict the understanding of socially and environmentally sustainable development built up over 30 years of experience, research, and evaluation.

Linear, "cause and effect" thinking contradicts the understanding of development as a complex process that occurs in open systems. Pressure to demonstrate, measure, and be accountable for impact has led donors to conceptualize, implement and evaluate programs using tools and methods which seek a linear cause and effect relationship between a problem and the identified "solution" to that problem. However, experience tells us that development is a complex process that takes place in circumstances where a program cannot be isolated from the various actors with which it will interact (for example, other donors, partner organizations, government departments, communities, organizations, and groups within the community). Nor can it be insulated from the factors by which it will be influenced (these include social, political, cultural, economic, historical, and environmental factors). While it is necessary to simplify to some extent in order to plan and implement programs, methodologically one needs to acknowledge the contextual reality of which programs are a part.

Bureaucratized programming contradicts the relationships, vision, and values of socially sustainable development. Donor efforts to measure, demonstrate, and be accountable for development impact have led to a reliance on logic-based approaches — requirements that a "logical framework" or "results chain" be prepared in the planning, management, and evaluation of each program. The state to which this practice has evolved has fostered a bureaucratization in programming. In his book, *Impact Assessment for Development Agencies*, Chris Roche identifies a trend in the way we conceptualize and plan for development. In this trend, "agreements and partnerships based on shared values have been replaced by bureaucratic trust based on plans, budgets, and accounts" (Roche 1999). This emphasis on plans, budgets, and accounts has implications for: how partners are selected; the ways in which relationships with partners develop; the kind of programs that are initiated; the ways in which those programs are designed and implemented; and the type of management and reporting that is expected of program partners. Overall, this shift in approach leads to structures that foster the belief among managers that appropriately completed and updated planning and reporting documents greatly increase the quality of development work, as well as increasing managers' influence over the achievement of results. While this may be true in a very limited sense, experience suggests that this approach reduces the likelihood of strong partnerships and stakeholder involvement. Shared vision, values, and commitment, risk-taking, innovation, and the seeking out of new partners are all incompatible with the domination of bureau-cratic instruments. Passion and a sense of purpose can easily be lost and, with them, opportunities for achieving sustained benefits.

Attribution of impact to donors contradicts the multiple endogenous contri-butions and conditions necessary for sustainable development. Even though it is commonly understood that socially sustainable development occurs when a variety of actors and factors converge to allow local organizations to take ownership and responsibility for planning and implementing program-ming, donors feel that it is necessary to be accountable for impact. They feel pressured to attribute to their interventions the changes that have occurred. In seeking to demonstrate how programs have led to development impact, one does not examine or learn about how the contributions or involvement of others (including donors, recipients, other organizations, and partici-pants), and the environment in which those interventions occur, fit together to create development results.

In particular, efforts to account for donor contributions to development impact ignore a key factor of socially sustainable development: the need for endogenous organizations and communities to take ownership of program components. Local ownership requires the devolution of planning, decision making, and other elements from external actors to internal actors. Yet, if one seeks to demonstrate how one's contribution led to development impact, one intentionally elevates that contribution above those of the other actors and factors that have played a part in developmental change. Using the simplified "results chain" model, Figure 2 illustrates the shifts in influ-ence as events move along the "results chain" towards impact.

Typically, at the "input" end of the process, the externally supported program has a great deal of control over decisions and events (such as budget and design, choice of partners, location, and timing). At this stage, the local partners and beneficiaries have the least influence. However, once funding flows, activities start, and local participants become increasingly active, the balance of influence should begin to change. If the program progresses as intended, local actors become more committed and their roles become more prominent. For the outcomes of the program to be relevant and lead to long-term, large-scale, sustainable benefits (in other words, to create impact), local ownership needs to become effective and dominant. This model suggests that the more successful the program, as it moves towards the impact stage, the more its exogenous influence is

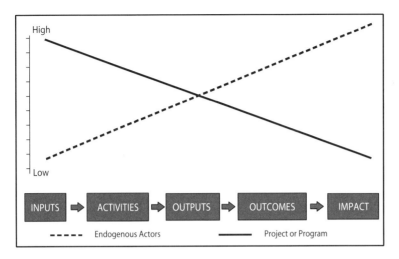

Figure 2. Relative Influence Along the Results Chain
(source: Smutylo 2001)

supplanted by endogenous activities and institutions. Thus a paradox exists for external agencies under pressure to take credit for results at the "impact" stage; for it is here, where their influence, if they have been successful, is low and decreasing relative to that of other actors.

The notion of program impact contradicts the ongoing confluence of initiatives and conditions that affect social and environmental well-being. The search for impact leads donors to look for and expect results at the end of each program. The intention is often to alter plans for further funding or implementation based on whether or not results are being achieved at certain points within the funding cycle. While it is appropriate to look for development results, in many cases these may not occur until some time after the program is completed. The desire to show measurable or actionable results can shorten the vision of an initiative to aim at goals that are attainable in the short term with very low risk.

Even in cases where it is realistic to look for development impact at the end of a single initiative, the story does not end once "impact" arrives. In IDRC's experience, whether the desired results are achieved or not, change continues. Conditions will perpetually be affected by combinations of social and natural events. Development does not occur in one, three, or five-year periods with a clear beginning, middle, and end. It is realistic, therefore, to expect that individual programs will make a difference that is incremental and cumulative rather than singular and dramatic. It is also reasonable to expect that even once the desired outcome has been reached, it may erode due to subsequent influences either within or entirely independent of the program. Aware of this reality, many development agencies seek to build endogenous capacity to maintain the ability to respond to ongoing changes.

Outcome Mapping deals with the problem of how to attribute impact by increasing the value and attention placed on results achieved "upstream" from impact. It does this by focusing on the changes that are clearly within a program's sphere of influence. While, at first glance, this appears to suggest concentrating on easier, less important, short-term achievements, in fact it does the opposite. It focuses attention on incremental, often subtle changes, without which the large-scale, more prominent achievements in human well-being cannot be attained or sustained.

Outcome Mapping focuses planning, monitoring, and evaluation on targeted behaviours, actions, and relationships within a program's sphere of influence, as well as on learning how to increase a program's effectiveness in relation to its ultimate goals. A corresponding change in reporting requirements would be for donors to make their recipients accountable for demonstrating that they are progressing towards impact and improving in their effectiveness — but not accountable for the impact itself. In this shift to accountability for learning, the connection between the results of a program's activities and the desired impact becomes rational, not empirical. The intended "impact" of the program is its guiding light and directional beacon, a test of its relevance — it is not the yardstick against which performance is measured. Thus the threat of failing to discover "hidden attribution" is eliminated when feedback on performance concentrates on improving rather than on proving, on understanding rather than on reporting, and on creating knowledge rather than on taking credit.

How Can Outcome Mapping Be Used?

Outcome Mapping is presented in this manual as an integrated planning, monitoring, and evaluation approach that is best used at the beginning of a program once the main focus of the program has been decided. Outcome Mapping is particularly effective when used from the planning stage, as it helps a program to focus on supporting specific changes in its partners. With some adaptations, its various elements and tools can be used separately or in conjunction with other processes (for example, a SWOT, a situational analysis, or an LFA). This manual does not provide the reader with instructions on how to adapt Outcome Mapping, but instead assumes it is being used in its totality. Outcome Mapping helps the program to clarify what it wants to accomplish, with whom, and how. It then offers a method for monitoring changes in the boundary partners and in the program as an organization, and encourages the program to look regularly at how it can improve its performance. It can also be used as an end-of-program assessment tool when the purpose of the evaluation is to study the program as a whole.

In Outcome Mapping, planning, monitoring, and evaluation are not discrete events but are designed to be cyclical, with one feeding into the other. It is impossible to plan for all eventualities, therefore a successful program is one that assesses and adapts to changing situations in an intelligent way, based on thoughtful reflection. Planning is done based on the best knowledge available, and the program uses monitoring and evaluation as reflective tools to assess change and choose appropriate actions.

Outcome Mapping can help a program tell its performance story by providing a framework for it to design and articulate its logic; record internal and external monitoring data; indicate cases of positive performance and areas for improvement; evaluate intended and unexpected results; gather data on its contribution to changes in its partners; and establish priorities and an evaluation plan. The framework helps the program to ask a series of questions, outlined below.

Designing and articulating the program's logic:

- What are our development goals?
- How can our program contribute to those development goals?
- Who are our boundary partners?
- How do we need to change in order to influence our boundary partners' contribution to the broader development goals?

Recording internal and external monitoring data:

- How far have our boundary partners progressed towards achieving outcomes?
- What are we doing to support the achievement of outcomes?
- How well have we performed?

Indicating cases of positive performance and areas for improvement:

- What worked well? Why? Are all the necessary strategies included?
- Are we spreading ourselves too thin by trying to use too many strategies?
- How can we maximize our contributions?

Evaluating intended and unexpected results:

- Who changed? How did they change?
- If they did not change as expected, do we need to do something different or reorient our expectations?

Gathering data on the contribution that a program made to bringing about changes in its partners:

- What activities/strategies were used?
- How did the activities influence individuals, groups, or institutions to change?

Establishing evaluation priorities and an evaluation plan:

- What strategies, relationships, or issues need to be studied in depth?
- How, and from where, can we gather relevant data?

Outcome Mapping can help a program to be more strategic about the actors it targets, the changes it expects to see, and the means it employs. It is designed to make the program more effective in terms of the results to which it contributes.

How Outcome Mapping Differs from Other Logic Models

Outcome Mapping provides a way to model what a program intends to do; however, it differs from most traditional logic models in a number of ways. Most significantly, Outcome Mapping recognizes that different boundary partners operate within different logic and responsibility systems. Outcome Mapping is not based on a cause–effect framework; rather, it recognizes that multiple, nonlinear events lead to change. It does not attempt to attribute outcomes to any single intervention or series of interventions. Instead, it looks at the logical links between interventions and behavioural change. By doing this, Outcome Mapping assumes only that a contribution has been made, and never attempts attribution.

In operational terms, this means that instead of attempting to monitor and evaluate all elements of the program with one set of tools, Outcome Mapping defines three distinct but highly interrelated sets of activities and changes, and offers tools to monitor each one. Thus, in addition to monitoring changes in boundary partners, it also monitors the program's strategies and organizational practices to enhance understanding of how the program has contributed to change. See Figure 3, below. As already discussed, if a program is to make a significant contribution, it needs to grow and develop so that it can constantly be improving its ability to work with its partners.

Figure 3. Spheres for Monitoring

Outcome Mapping has expanded the "reach" concept into a performance area by moving from a conceptual understanding of intermediate impacts to a focus on the change process in boundary partners (using outcome challenge statements and progress markers).[1] Although other logic models may include changes in behaviour as a part of their framework, Outcome Mapping focuses exclusively on changes in the behaviour of those individuals, groups, and organizations with whom a program works directly. This does not mean that other social, environmental, economic, or political changes should not be measured, but that is not the

---

[1] The "reach" concept was originally introduced to IDRC through Steve Montague in the early 1990s as an output measure of the scope of a project or program. The concept evolved to be understood as a dimension of impact, because it dealt with the uptake or adoption of research findings. For further information, see Sander (1998).

focus of Outcome Mapping. It monitors and evaluates whether a program has contributed to changes in behaviours in a way that would be logically consistent with supporting development changes in the future. By focusing on this level of change, it assesses the work of the program under review, and is not limited to the end state of the context in which the boundary partners operate. Therefore, programs get credit not only for being present when a major development change occurs, but for their ongoing contributions to that change.

Outcome Mapping recognizes challenges beyond the scope of the program, but limits performance assessment to the program's direct sphere of influence. In this way, it pushes the program toward increased risk-taking, with the view that risk-taking is a necessary condition for encouraging development. Most logical frameworks tend to limit vision and scope by expressly linking a program's modest activities to a development impact. This significantly reduces the potential for significant contributions to development by forcing the program to link each activity causally to a measurable result.

By linking organizational assessment with the monitoring of changes in boundary partners, Outcome Mapping recognizes that the program will also have to change during the course of an initiative. If the program is unwilling or incapable of recognizing and adapting to the roles of its boundary partners, then it will eventually defeat its very purpose for being. Outcome Mapping encourages a program to think of itself as a dynamic organization whose goals, methods, and relationships with partners need to be reconsidered and adjusted regularly.

When Is Outcome Mapping Best Used?

Once a program has established its strategic directions or primary program areas, Outcome Mapping helps sort out who is going to be affected, in what ways, and through what activities on the program's part. It then permits a program to design a monitoring and evaluation system to help document and manage outcomes.

Once programming areas are chosen, Outcome Mapping can be used at two levels. At the **project level**, it is particularly effective in planning, monitoring, and evaluating large projects. Small projects rarely require the level of detail that Outcome Mapping provides. It is best used from the start of a project, but can also be used as an assessment tool (for external or self-assessment) either during or at the end of a project. If used after a project is underway, it will usually require a reformulation of vision, mission, boundary partners, and outcome challenge statements, as few project statements can be directly translated into behavioural terms without consultation among the key participants.

Outcome Mapping can also be used at the **program level**, but it often requires that the program organize its activities in terms of its sub-programming areas. For example, a program on urban agriculture could be divided into waste-water reuse and confined space agriculture areas. At too high a level of generality, it is difficult to identify who will change and how they will change, thereby reducing the likelihood of success. A program must be sufficiently specific for the group to be able to identify key groups who will be influenced. At both levels, Outcome Mapping requires that groups be able to name identifiable partners whose behaviours should be influenced by the activities of the project or program.

Is Outcome Mapping Appropriate for You?

Outcome Mapping is not necessarily the appropriate methodology for all programs, as it may require a change in perspective and approach that is not possible. The program needs to be able to focus on outcomes — defined as changes in the behaviours, relationships, activities, or actions of the people, groups, and organizations with whom it works directly. Outcome Mapping also involves a commitment to change on the part of the program, and self-assessment is an integral element of the methodology. In order to assess whether Outcome Mapping is appropriate for a program, the group should consider the following issues.

Strategic Directions Defined

Outcome Mapping is best used once a program has made a decision about its strategic directions or primary program areas. It does not provide a means to prioritize or select programming niches. Outcome Mapping helps sort out what, in operational terms, the strategic plan means: who is going to be affected, in what ways, and through what program activities. It then permits a program to design a monitoring and evaluation system to help track intended outcomes.

Type of Monitoring and Evaluation Information Sought

Outcome Mapping can provide information for a particular type of evaluation study — one that looks at the program's performance or the outcomes achieved by its partners. It is not intended for a technical evaluation to assess the relevance of the programming area or an evaluation of the cost-effectiveness of one approach compared with another.

Reporting Requirements

Outcome Mapping depends largely on self-assessment data generated systematically by the program team and the boundary partners. It requires a commitment to participatory and learning-based approaches to monitoring and evaluation. Although the approach can be modified to include an external assessment, the program should ensure that the data collected meets its formal reporting requirements and that its managers or donors consider it sufficiently credible. This should be done before starting the process to ensure its utility.

Team Consensus

Ideally, the team shares an understanding of the purpose of their work, works collaboratively, and values each other's opinions. If this is not the case and there is disagreement among team members, Outcome Mapping is not the magic bullet that will solve all the problems. It can, however, provide an opportunity for the group to discuss and negotiate viewpoints systematically and move towards consensus.

Resource Commitments

The program has to be willing to commit the financial, human, and time resources necessary to design and implement a monitoring and evaluation system. A design workshop takes approximately three days. The monitoring system will take one staff member about one day per monitoring session. A few hours will be required from each of the other staff members to contribute data.

2 OUTCOME MAPPING: THE WORKSHOP APPROACH

The tools and methods of Outcome Mapping as presented here are designed for use in a facilitated three-day workshop. This chapter outlines the basic steps and outputs of the workshop, discusses who should participate, and offers suggestions on how to facilitate the workshop and use the tools provided in the manual.

Overview of the Steps

There are three stages and twelve steps to Outcome Mapping. They take the program from reaching consensus about the macro-level changes it would like to support to developing a monitoring framework and an evaluation plan. The 12 steps are shown on the next page. The process is participatory so that, once members of the program articulate their intentions, decide on strategies, develop a monitoring system, and identify evaluation priorities and data collection needs together, they will share ownership and commitment for the entire enterprise and can integrate it into their daily programming activities and management.

The twelve steps are the elements of an Outcome Mapping design workshop. The first stage, **Intentional Design**, helps a program clarify and establish consensus regarding the macro-level changes it would like to support. Intentional design is carried out only once a program has chosen its strategic directions and wants to chart its goals, partners, activities, and progress towards anticipated results. After clarifying the changes the program intends to help bring about, activities are chosen that maximize the likelihood of success. The Intentional Design stage helps answer four questions: **Why?** (vision statement); **Who?** (boundary partners); **What?** (outcome challenges and progress markers); and **How?** (mission, strategy maps, organizational practices).

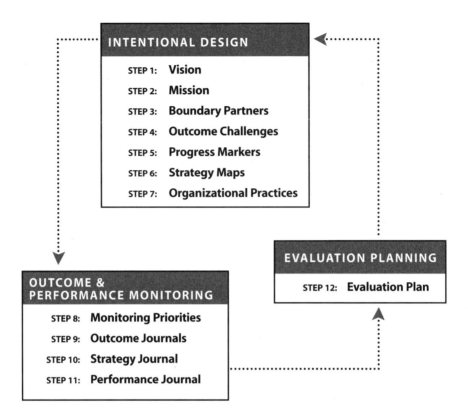

The second stage, **Outcome & Performance Monitoring**, helps a program clarify its monitoring and evaluation priorities. It provides a framework for ongoing monitoring of the program's actions in support of its boundary partners' progress towards the achievement of outcomes, the strategies the program has employed to foster those changes, and its organizational practices. The program uses progress markers — a set of graduated indicators of the behavioural change identified in the intentional design stage — to clarify directions with boundary partners and to monitor outcomes. It uses the strategy maps and organizational practices to create a performance monitoring framework. If completed regularly, this framework gives the program the opportunity and tools both to reflect on and improve its performance, and to collect data on the results of its work with its boundary partners.

Whereas, using the monitoring framework in Stage Two, the program gathers information that is broad in coverage, the evaluations planned in Stage Three assess a strategy, issue, or relationship in greater depth. This stage, **Evaluation Planning**, helps the program set evaluation priorities so that it can target evaluation resources and activities where they will be most useful. An evaluation plan outlines the main elements of the evaluations to be conducted and, finally, an evaluation design is presented. It should be noted that Outcome Mapping provides a method to frame, organize, and collect data, but it does not analyze the information. The program will still need to interpret the data in order to make it useful for learning and improvement or to share its experiences or results with others. Although all elements of Outcome Mapping (such as progress markers and strategy maps) can be used independently, this manual is set up as though the program were using the full approach from the outset, as established through a workshop process.

Workshop Outputs

The outputs of an Outcome Mapping design workshop include:

- A brief representation of the logic of the macro-level changes to which the program wants to contribute (vision, mission, boundary partners, and outcome challenges);
- A set of strategy maps outlining the program's activities in support of each outcome (strategy maps);
- A change ladder for each boundary partner to monitor the progress towards the achievement of outcomes (progress markers, outcome journal);
- A self-assessment sheet for monitoring what the program is doing internally to manage its work and contribute to change in its boundary partners (organizational practices, performance journal);
- A data collection sheet for data on the strategies being employed by the program to encourage change in the boundary partner (strategy journal); and
- An evaluation plan detailing: the priority evaluation topics, issues, and questions; a utilization strategy for the evaluation findings; the person responsible for conducting the evaluation; the date; and the cost (evaluation plan).

Who Should Participate?

The workshop method presented in this manual is most appropriate for a group of 18 to 25 participants. If there are more participants, the facilitator will have to adjust the process to include more small group and plenary activities. Testing of Outcome Mapping to date has been with people who are educated and are comfortable and confident expressing themselves orally in front of a group. The groups have also been relatively free of conflict, as it has been tested with people who share a common cause (for example, those working in an organizational or program setting). If this is not the case, the facilitator will most likely have to adjust the process to fit the culture, skills, and dynamics of the group.

Outcome Mapping, as a participatory process, can ideally involve the full range of stakeholders, including staff from the program, boundary partners, donors, and ultimate beneficiaries. It is, however, premised on the belief that responsibility for planning, monitoring, and evaluation should rest primarily with program staff. This is because, ultimately, they are responsible for the program, need to learn how to better serve their boundary partners, and must fulfill their reporting requirements. This does not mean that boundary partners cannot or should not be incorporated into the process. However, there are no concrete rules about who should participate in each stage, and this will need to be considered by the program on an iterative basis.

The planning, monitoring, and evaluation of a program benefits from the participation of boundary partners. Participation in the Outcome Mapping design workshop by boundary partners may be an opportunity for frank and open dialogue or negotiation about the purpose and relevance of the program. It may also offer a way in which decisions can be made consultatively about how the program will be implemented and assessed. Nonetheless, genuine participation is not simple in the context of an externally funded development program. Donor agencies wanting to use participatory approaches need to be aware of the power imbalance that necessarily exists between the agency managing the program and any beneficiaries or partner groups who are expected to participate. Participation should be requested in a spirit of equitable collaboration, and the complexity of existing relationships should be considered in each instance. Whether the boundary partner is a recipient of funding or not, the program should also consider what that partner will get out of participating. Is it useful for the partner? The program could ask itself at various stages, "How can our program be open, consultative, and transparent with our boundary partners while being realistic about their desire and ability to participate fully?"

There may be cases where the participation of boundary partners in a program's Outcome Mapping workshop may not be necessary or useful. Participation of boundary partners needs to be considered on a case-by-case basis. When deciding who should participate in the Outcome Mapping workshop, the program should consider:

- What they can contribute to the discussion (What is their perspective on, relationship to, or interest in the program? Are all the viewpoints and expertise necessary to make informed decisions present?);
- Whether they can effectively participate in the discussion (Are there any barriers in terms of language, substantive knowledge of the programming area, hierarchy, or politics?);
- What they will get out of participating in the design workshop;
- Whether information from them is better gathered prior to the workshop and then fed into the discussion (Will their participation hinder the openness and honesty of the conversation?);
- Whether the necessary time, human, and financial resources are available; and
- Whether the timing and location of the meeting(s) fit their schedule.

Who Should Facilitate?

A facilitator who is familiar with the Outcome Mapping methodology and comfortable with the concepts of evaluation for learning, participatory research, and organizational change should lead the workshop. This may be either an internal or external facilitator. The role of the facilitator is to engage participants, ensure that all opinions are heard and considered, note areas of consensus and differences, and keep the discussion moving so that the group can complete its task in the time allotted. Therefore, the individual should be skilled in consensus building, be able to determine the power dynamics in a group, and be able to ensure that the diverse opinions of the group are captured.

There are advantages and disadvantages to both internal and external facilitators. An outsider can ask the basic questions that will force the group to reflect on, and be very clear about, the purpose of the program. Using an external facilitator can also allow the entire group to concentrate on the substance of the meeting. Nonetheless, external facilitators can be costly and, unless the outsider understands the substance of the programming area, the group may have to provide detailed background information and explanation to enable effective facilitation. On the other hand, having an internal facilitator means that one member of the group will not be able to contribute fully to the substantive discussions. A good option is to team an internal team member with an external facilitator. This can be especially useful if the program plans to facilitate Outcome Mapping sessions itself at a later date.

Workshop Materials

This manual presents the elements of the Outcome Mapping methodology as they proceed from design to monitoring to evaluation. In Sections Three, Four, and Five, each step of Outcome Mapping is discussed, a group process is outlined, and an example of the finished "products" is provided.

This manual offers suggestions and tips for running the workshop, but these are not intended to be a rigid set of activities that must be followed lockstep. There are many different ways to facilitate groups, and the processes provided in this manual are the ones that, based on IDRC's experiences, have worked well in development research organizations. The facilitator should be flexible and employ the methods that work best in their specific context.

Presentation Methods

If available, an LCD projector can be used throughout the twelve steps of Outcome Mapping to project the group's thoughts and ideas onto a screen as the facilitator enters them into the computer. This immediate feedback promotes a common language among the participants and allows them to easily review and revise their vision, mission, list of boundary partners, outcome challenge statements, progress markers, strategy maps, organizational practices, monitoring journals, and evaluation plan. It also makes the workshop documentation available immediately to the participants. It is helpful if the information is printed and distributed to participants at each step so that they can consult it throughout the process. This approach can also slow down the discussion slightly and give participants an opportunity to reflect while the facilitator is typing. The disadvantage of this facilitation method is that if the group is not used to the technology, participants can be distracted by it. If this is the case, flip charts are a better alternative — although the facilitator should ensure that the material generated at each step remains displayed in the room so that it can be consulted throughout the process.

Simultaneously facilitating and typing information into a laptop is difficult when working with a large group. If the facilitator cannot see the entire group while seated at the computer, then (s)he will have trouble watching and responding to the group. The facilitator should have experience and be very comfortable with using the laptop and LCD projector, otherwise the session can be held up by technical problems, which is very frustrating.

Although the setup of the room is dependent on its shape and the number of participants, the participants should all be able to view one another and speak easily. There should be a large empty wall where information can be posted either on small cards or on flip chart paper. Generally, a U-shaped arrangement works well. The facilitator should have the room prepared before the group arrives.

The items required to facilitate an Outcome Mapping design workshop using the process proposed in this manual include

- Paper and pens
- 8 ½ x 5" cards
- Markers
- Masking tape
- Flip charts

Preparing for an Outcome Mapping Workshop

Outcome Mapping requires a change in thinking about what constitutes results. Therefore it is advisable to have an introductory presentation on the theory of the methodology prior to the actual design workshop. Some programs will want more background on the methodology than others. Nonetheless, explaining it prior to the workshop can make the steps easier to move through. As the facilitator plans the agenda and timing of the workshop, (s)he should assemble and adapt the materials that seem most appropriate to the needs of the group.

The following two activities may be used before the workshop or as it begins, depending on the needs of participants and the stage of their program:

- A historical scanning activity that reviews the program's history and the events and issues that have influenced its development to date; and
- An activity designed to help participants reach consensus about their understanding of evaluation.

Conducting a Historical Scan

Purpose: When beginning a program planning process, it can be useful for a group **to review the program's history, its achievements, and the events and issues that have influenced its development to date.** If the program has been active and is entering a new phase, this "warm-up" exercise can help contextualize the events and influencing factors for both new and seasoned staff. It can also give a group the opportunity to develop a shared understanding of the past and a common language with which to discuss the future.

Process

Approximate Time	3 hours

ICA (Institute of Cultural Affairs) Canada (n.d.) has developed a participatory approach for a group to conduct a quick historical scan. As many members of the program team as possible should participate in this brainstorming activity, outlined below.

1. The facilitator asks each member of the group to write down an answer to the following question: "What are the key events (positive or negative milestones) in the past X years that were important to you? Professionally? Organizationally? Nationally? Globally/Internationally? Personally?" The amount of time, X, will vary but can be determined by the length of time the program has been operating. For example, a program that is planning for its second five-year cycle could cover the five or six previous years.

2. On the wall, the facilitator makes a time line, dividing it vertically by time and horizontally by type of event (events that relate to the organization, national events, and international events).

Depending on the length of time the group has to cover, the time period can be divided various ways (monthly, quarterly, semi-annually, annually, biannually, and so on).

3. As participants call out events, the facilitator puts them on the time line. The discussion regarding the timing of events and their significance is an essential part of this exercise, so the group should be left to work this through.

4. Once the events have all been put up on the time line, the facilitator gets the group to analyze their overall meaning by asking them questions that encourage them to look at the data from different perspectives. The facilitator should capture the participants' comments on a flip chart, but most of the agreement and learning will probably result from the discussions rather than the facilitator's notes. The facilitator asks the following questions to begin the discussion:

   - What are the high/low points or successes/challenges?
   - Where are the shifts or turning points? What kind? Why?
   - How would you name the earlier/mid/later periods (chronologically/vertically)?
   - What trends/issues do you see over the period? Vertically? Horizontally?

Developing a Common Understanding of Evaluation

Purpose: Before beginning the Outcome Mapping steps, engaging the group in a short discussion on evaluation can encourage them to create a common language for the duration of the workshop and ensure that everyone understands the evaluation approach being proposed.

Process	**Approximate Time**	**30 min.**

Everyone has preconceived ideas about evaluation — some positive, some negative. Although it is possible that some participants think of evaluation as useful, many more probably have negative perceptions, are fearful of the process, or view evaluation as having limited utility. The facilitator needs to be aware of these opinions and build on, or respond to, them throughout the workshop. Because Outcome Mapping integrates monitoring and evaluation issues from a program's earliest planning stage, the staff will not be passive recipients who are fed information and reports. Rather, they will be active contributors from the outset. Therefore the facilitator needs to create a participatory environment in which everyone feels comfortable, able, and interested in contributing. This will be accomplished primarily through actions rather than words. That is, the facilitator's actions will demonstrate that (s)he is an active listener who remains neutral. However, it can be useful to have the group engage in a short discussion on the topic before beginning the Outcome Mapping steps. This will allow the group to create a common language for the workshop. Michael Quinn Patton suggests one technique for organizing this type of discussion (Patton 1997):

1. The facilitator asks each member of the group to write down the first three words or images they associate with the word "evaluation." They are given only a few minutes, so that their emotional responses come out.

2. People call out the words they wrote down and the facilitator records them on a flip chart. Some of the words may have a positive connotation (such as "interesting" and "enjoyment"), some may have a neutral connotation (such as "research" or "test"), and some may have a negative connotation (such as "pain," "fear," "manipulation," or "judgement").

3. The facilitator asks the group how the words make them feel: Do they find any of the words surprising? If so, participants can discuss why they are surprised to see certain words or types of words associated with evaluation. Do they feel that others in the group have the same impressions as they do about evaluation? Why? Why not?

4. The facilitator asks the group how they would like their program's evaluation process to proceed. Based on the previous discussions, which characteristics do they want included? What do they want to avoid? This information should be captured on a flip chart and can be used later in the workshop as a checklist for assessing workshop outputs.

5. Once the participants have expressed their opinions, the facilitator responds by talking about his or her role and suggesting a way for the workshop process to proceed. This conversation should continue until there is agreement between the facilitator and the group on how they will proceed. The list of guiding principles for evaluation at IDRC (next page) can offer the facilitator some ideas about issues to highlight in this exercise or can be passed out to participants.

FACILITATION TIP

The facilitator's actions will set the tone for the workshop, therefore the facilitator should try to create a climate of trust and mutual respect by letting participants know that there are no right or wrong answers and that everyone has information and opinions that will make the process and product better (the whole is greater than the sum of its parts).

Guiding Principles for Evaluation

At IDRC, evaluation is viewed as an integral part of good project and program management. Corporate and program learning and improvement drives evaluation activities, with collegial participation by stakeholders as a key ingredient. IDRC has chosen to use evaluation first as a corporate learning tool, believing this to be the best way to strengthen its accountability function. The following principles, which guide evaluation at IDRC, are embedded in the process of Outcome Mapping and argue for the relevance of evaluation as an integral component of a program's learning system:

- **Evaluation is intended to improve program planning and delivery** — It contributes to decision making and strategy formulation at all levels. To increase the likelihood of obtaining useful findings, programs are assessed strategically, based on the client's purpose and information needs.

- **Evaluations are designed to lead to action** — To be useful, evaluations need to produce relevant, action-oriented findings. This is fostered by sustained involvement and ownership on the part of the client and stakeholders throughout the process.

- **No single, best, generic evaluation method exists** — Each case requires tools and methods appropriate to the data that is to be gathered and analyzed, and appropriate to the client's needs. Credible evaluations interlace quantitative and qualitative data from several sources.

- **Evaluations should enlist the participation of relevant stakeholders** — Those affected by the outcome of an evaluation have a right to be involved in the process. Their participation will help them to better understand the evaluation's purpose and process, and will promote stakeholder contribution to, and acceptance of, the evaluation results. This increases the likelihood that evaluation findings will be utilized.

- **Evaluation processes should meet standards for ethical research** — Participants in the process should be able to act and share information fully without fear that the information they provide could be used against them at a later time.

- **Monitoring and evaluation planning add value at the design stage of a program** — They can make the program more efficient and effective by helping to clarify the results to be achieved. Also, knowing what information will be used will allow people to collect it as it becomes available. This will reduce the amount of financial and human resources required and improve the team's ability to report on, and learn from, its experiences.

- **Evaluation should be an asset for those being evaluated** — Evaluation can impose a considerable time and resource burden on recipient institutions. Evaluations should generate information that benefits the recipient institution.

- **Evaluation is both science and art** — The art of identifying critical issues to be evaluated, organizing them conceptually, and getting the appropriate people to participate in the collection, interpretation, and utilization of the evaluation information is as important as the systematic collection and analysis of reliable data.

- **Evaluations are a means of negotiating different realities** — Evaluations provide opportunities for program stakeholders to reconcile their various perspectives or versions of reality.

- **Evaluations should leave behind an increased capacity to use evaluation findings** — Organizations need some level of internal evaluation capacity in order to be able to devise, participate in, or utilize evaluations effectively. Exclusive reliance on external expertise can limit an organization's ability to be clear and specific about its goals and to learn and apply lessons. Specific strategies can be built into evaluations that are aimed explicitly at fostering these organizational characteristics.

3 STAGE1: INTENTIONAL DESIGN

INTENTIONAL DESIGN

STEP 1: **Vision**

STEP 2: **Mission**

STEP 3: **Boundary Partners**

STEP 4: **Outcome Challenges**

STEP 5: **Progress Markers**

STEP 6: **Strategy Maps**

STEP 7: **Organizational Practices**

OUTCOME & PERFORMANCE MONITORING

STEP 8: **Monitoring Priorities**

STEP 9: **Outcome Journals**

STEP 10: **Strategy Journal**

STEP 11: **Performance Journal**

EVALUATION PLANNING

STEP 12: **Evaluation Plan**

Introduction to Stage 1

Intentional design implies that a program frames its activities based on the changes it intends to help bring about and that its actions are purposely chosen so as to maximize the effectiveness of its contributions to development. During the intentional design stage, workshop participants define the development goals of the program. The logic of the program is articulated by following seven steps to outline the vision, mission, boundary partners, outcome challenges, graduated progress markers, strategy maps, and organizational practices.

The vision statement describes why the program is engaged in development and provides an inspirational focus. Workshop participants are encouraged to be truly visionary in Step 1, establishing a vivid beacon to motivate staff and highlight the ultimate purpose of their day-to-day work. The boundary partners (those with whom the program will work directly) are identified so that they can contribute to the vision. The outcome challenge statements and progress markers identify the results that the program would like to see its boundary partners achieve. The mission, strategy maps, and organizational practices describe how the program's contributions to the vision will be framed, by focusing on what it will do. By working its way through the seven steps, the program articulates how it will contribute to change within the complex system in which it operates.

Defining the elements of the intentional design stage is easiest if the members of the program already have a shared understanding of the ultimate purpose of their work. This consensus may be the result of a formal process or of informal discussions. Regardless, it makes the articulation of a vision and mission quite straightforward. If there is not consensus, and the group is using Outcome Mapping to negotiate various perspectives, options, and scenarios, then the intentional design stage may take longer to develop. Nonetheless, appropriate effort should be devoted to this "visioning" stage because, if properly articulated in the beginning, the vision's elements should remain relevant for the duration of the program (three to five years).

STEP 1
Describe the Vision

EXAMPLE OF A VISION STATEMENT

In the medium and large cities of Africa, the Middle East, and Latin America, the value of urban agriculture (UA) as an integral part of effective urban management and development is recognized by local authorities, communities, and international organizations. Municipal, regional, and national governments actively support UA activities by formulating and implementing UA-related policies. Using research findings, these governments have developed a comprehensive urban food supply and security strategy that allows cities to fully exploit their local strengths and create effective mechanisms for collaboration with rural and regional agriculture production sectors. More green spaces are built into cities, including designated areas for fruit trees, which provide shade and help to purify the air. To be more resource efficient, cities treat and reuse waste water for irrigating crops and watering livestock. Farms and households compost organic matter and recycle waste, contributing to better urban sanitation. Urban dwellers have greater food security, and more self-reliant local food systems are in place. Men and women who want to engage in UA have access to land and technical information so as to reduce their food insecurity and generate income. Producers, both rural and urban, have easy access to urban markets, as they are supported by a reliable physical infrastructure and are well organized. They are able to sell their products for a fair profit. Formerly marginalized producers are organized into advocacy groups that can effectively present their needs to policymakers. All groups have access to reliable and relevant technical information about UA. In essence, these cities are better fed, healthier, wealthier, more equitable, and cleaner.

The vision reflects the large-scale development-related changes that the program hopes to encourage. It describes economic, political, social, or environmental changes that the program hopes to help bring about, as well as broad behavioural changes in key boundary partners. The vision is related to the program's objectives but goes deeper, is broader in scope, and is longer-term. The ultimate achievement of the vision lies beyond the program's capability; however, its activities should contribute to and facilitate that end. It is the program's contribution toward the vision (through its boundary partners) that will be measured in an evaluation — not whether the vision was achieved. The vision represents the ideal that the program wants to support and should be sufficiently broad and inspirational to remain relevant over time, despite changing circumstances. The facilitator should return to the vision statement over the course of the planning exercise to ensure that the program's activities are consistent with its intent.

Depending on the complexity of its programming, a program can use Outcome Mapping at different levels. For example, an organization or large program might want to articulate a vision and mission for its overall work and for each of its programming areas. A relatively contained program, on the other hand, would probably only need to develop one vision and mission statement.

The vision statement can be recorded on Design Worksheet 1 on page 51.

Process
Approximate Time 2 hours

1. As a warm-up discussion, the facilitator asks a member of the group to respond to the following question: "In just a few sentences, what is this program supposed to accomplish?" The facilitator then involves the entire group in the discussion by asking, "Is this the way everyone sees the program? Does this fit with our organization's objectives and mandate?"

2. The facilitator then has each participant write down the two to three characteristics that would describe the near future (the next three to five years) if the program was wildly successful, asking the following questions: "What are your dreams of success? What changes do you want to try to help bring about? Imagine the context in three to five years when the program has been very successful: what would be different?" The facilitator posts the answers on the wall and the group reviews and discusses them.

3. While the group is on a break, the facilitator (alone or with volunteer participant(s)) writes up a vision statement that uses the participants' ideas and language, eliminates duplication, and captures differences.

4. Once the group has reconvened, the vision statement is revised. Politically charged, culturally inappropriate, or incorrect statements are removed and jargon or confusing terms are replaced, using a process such as the following:

   a. The facilitator slowly reads the draft vision statement, asking team members to note any words or phrases that seem to be culturally insensitive or politically charged; jargon or potentially confusing; unnecessarily long-winded; or grammatically incorrect. On the first reading, it is best not to let anyone interrupt, so that the whole picture is presented at once, both in spoken word and visually on the LCD or flip chart.

b. The facilitator then reads the statement a second time, asking participants to interrupt if a word or phrase is read that is culturally inappropriate or politically charged. If a hand is raised, the problem area is discussed and an attempt is made to remedy it with alternative wording. Rather than the facilitator reading the vision statement each time, different participants should read it aloud as it is being revised.

c. When the wording is resolved, the facilitator continues reading. This procedure is followed until no culturally insensitive, politically charged, or incorrect words or phrases remain, yet ensuring that the vision reflects participants' intentions.

5. As an alternative to Step 4b, the troublesome words or phrases are underlined and the reading continues. When the reading of the statement has been completed, the words or phrases that have been underlined are transferred to the top line of the "purging the jargon chart." If there are more than five such words or phrases, the ones that appear most significant to the team are selected. For each word or phrase selected, the facilitator asks participants to call out other ways of saying the same thing (without reference to the full statement). The choices (not limited to exact synonyms) are listed on the chart.

PURGING THE JARGON CHART

0	rural peasants	innovatively	sustainable development	profitable	vitality
1	rural poor	with	attention to imagination	money-making environment	prosperity
2	farmers	taking risks	protection of resources	worth doing	health
3	farm workers	creatively	long-term development	job-generating and income-producing	energy level
4	villagers	in new ways	holistic development	competitive	optimism

Source: Kibel, B.; Baretto, T.; Dieng, M.; Ndiaye, A.; Carden, F.; Earl, S. July 1999. Draft Outcome Engineering Manual.

6. The facilitator reads the part of the statement that contains the first word or phrase that was found lacking, each time substituting one of the alternatives from the chart. When all the options have been read, the facilitator asks the team members to vote by a show of hands for the variation they like best (including the original wording). If there is a clear majority, that option is substituted; if not, the facilitator leads a discussion of the options. On a re-vote, the option with the highest number of votes is selected. The process is repeated for the other words or phrases on the chart. The selected words or phrases are then substituted in the vision statement.

7. At the end of the process, the facilitator reads the entire vision statement aloud without interruption. It should evoke a spontaneous expression of approval from the group: people should feel that it reflects the broad development changes the program is trying to help bring about.

STEP 2
Identify the Mission

EXAMPLE OF A MISSION STATEMENT

In support of the vision, the program will work to enhance specific research expertise and training capacities in urban agriculture (UA) in research organizations that can influence local, national, and international policy-making in UA. It will contribute to the development of active networks of researchers and advocates and encourage partnerships between research organizations and interested governments. Working also with NGOs, government agencies, community groups, and other donors, it will support research to: document municipal practices and policies; test policy consultations; compare policy approaches in support of UA; and issue guidelines for incorporating UA into policies dealing with food supply and security, urban planning, gender inequality, poverty reduction, and waste management. It will encourage the identification of unresolved issues and will support research on these issues, for greater incorporation of UA into policy-making locally, regionally, nationally, and internationally. It will contribute to the production, organization and dissemination of data and information that will sensitize local and international actors to the positive and negative aspects of UA activities.

The mission statement describes how the program intends to support the vision. It states the areas in which the program will work toward the vision, but does not list all the activities in which the program will engage. Rather, it is an ideal statement about how the program will contribute. It represents what the program wants to grow into as it supports the achievement of the vision.

When drafting its mission statement, the group should consider not only how the program will support the achievement of outcomes by its boundary partners, but also how it will keep itself effective, efficient, and relevant. The manner in which it operates, uses information, and handles change plays a key role in determining how well it can carry out its activities. This is discussed in greater detail in Step 7 (organizational practices).

> The mission statement can be recorded on Design Worksheet 1 on page 51.

Process

Approximate Time 2 hours

1. The facilitator asks a member of the group to respond to the question, "How can the program best contribute to or support the achievement of the vision?" In other words, what does the program need to be like in order to support the vision? The facilitator then involves the entire group in the discussion by asking, "Is this the way everyone sees the mission of your work?"

2. The facilitator then has each participant write down two or three characteristics that the program would have if it was working ideally.

3. While the group is on a break, the facilitator (alone or with volunteer participant(s)) writes up a mission statement that uses the participants' ideas and language, eliminates duplication, and captures differences.

4. Once the group has reconvened, the mission statement is reviewed and revised.

5. At the end of the process, the facilitator reads the entire mission statement. It should evoke a spontaneous expression of approval from the group.

- Details regarding the program's mission are sometimes given when the group is describing its vision. If this occurs, the facilitator lists the information about the program's contributions under a separate heading called "Mission." Once the vision has been created, the facilitator reviews the elements of the mission with the group and refines it as required.

- While it is preferable to carry out the first two steps in a group setting, the facilitator can save time during the design workshop by asking participants to answer questions by e-mail in advance in order to draft the vision and mission statements. The drafts can then be revised when the entire group has assembled in the workshop. An example of such an e-mail "survey" is included on the next page. If written material from the program's staff seems to be contradictory, the facilitator should not attempt a synthesis, but rather start fresh in the workshop, where the whole group is present to express and discuss different viewpoints. Even when there is a strong convergence of views in the e-mail survey, the group exercise should still be given the time needed for participants to develop a common language. This is time well spent and will serve the group well for the rest of the workshop.

Hello!

Please answer each of the questions below so that I can draft a vision and mission statement for us to go over as a group. You can use point form if that is easier. Nobody will be identified by name, so please feel free to be idealistic and visionary.

Here are the questions:

1. Picture the program three to five years from now and imagine that it has been extremely successful in developing and implementing its activities. In this ideal situation, assuming everything went well, what changes did your program help to bring about? What have your partners achieved? What are they doing differently? In other words, what would total success look like?

2. How can the program best contribute to this vision? What areas does it need to work in to promote and support the realization of the vision? What does it need to do in these areas? What does it need to accomplish in these areas?

3. What individuals, organizations, or groups will the program need to work with to effect these changes? Who will you work with most directly? Who can help or hinder your work? Who are the ultimate beneficiaries?

4. Please state why these individuals, organizations, or groups are needed as partners.

If you could return your answers to me by Thursday, February 8, then I can draft the statements before our meeting early in the week of February 12. If you have any concerns or comments about the questions, please get in touch with me.

Looking forward to working together.

STEP 3
Identify the Boundary Partners

EXAMPLES OF BOUNDARY PARTNERS

1. Local communities (NGOs, indigenous groups, churches, community leaders, model forest administration unit)

2. Government officials and policymakers (national forestry agency/department, regional administration)

3. Private sector (tourism, fisheries, non-timber forest products, logging and wood processing companies)

4. Academic and research institutions

5. International institutions

Boundary partners are those individuals, groups, or organizations with whom the program interacts directly and with whom the program can anticipate opportunities for influence. These actors are called boundary partners because, even though the program will work with them to effect change, it does not control them. The power to influence development rests with them. The program is on the boundary of their world. The program tries to facilitate the process by providing access to new resources, ideas, or opportunities for a certain period of time. A single boundary partner may include multiple individuals, groups, or organizations if a similar change is being sought in all (for example, research centres or women's NGOs). Figure 4 illustrates the relationship of the program to its boundary partners, and the relationship of those actors to the broader environment in which development occurs.

When listing the program's boundary partners, the focus should be on the actors with whom it works directly. If the program cannot directly influence an actor, the group needs to determine who it can influence who will, in turn, influence that actor. The actor who can be influenced is then included as a boundary partner instead. In this way, the program maintains a focus on its sphere of influence, but with a broader vision. For example, a rural development NGO may not be able to influence the Minister of Finance directly, but it can influence farmer organizations, which can then lobby the Ministry to effect change. Therefore, the farmer organizations would be included in the NGO's list of boundary partners, but the Minister of Finance would not.

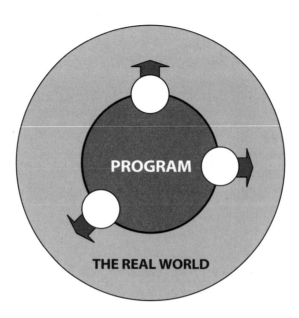

Figure 4. Boundary Partners
◯ = Program's Boundary Partners

Generally, a program does not have more than four or five types of boundary partners (although each boundary partner can include multiple individuals, groups, or organizations). When deciding how to group the individuals, groups, and organizations with whom the program works, the crucial feature is that the program truly wants to encourage changes in the behaviour, relationships, activities, or actions of that partner. For example, a rural development NGO may be working with five different farmer organizations in five provinces, but, if the changes that it is trying to help bring about in those organizations are the same, then they are grouped together as a single type of boundary partner.

If there are other actors that the program needs to work with but does not necessarily want to change, they can be listed separately under "strategic partners" so that they can later be considered when developing strategies. Other donors would most likely fit into this category. The program may want, or need, an alliance with them to achieve its objectives, but it is not trying to change their behaviour. Strategic partners are considered in terms of their contribution to the mission.

Figure 5 presents a typology of the actors whom IDRC-supported programs influence to act in ways consistent with sustainable and equitable development. In other words, these are the actors among whom

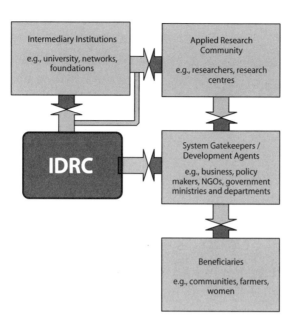

Figure 5. Typology of IDRC Boundary Partners
(source: Kibel 1999)

IDRC tries to encourage outcomes that contribute to its vision. Rather than being linear, the activities and relationships are dialogical, therefore the arrows go in both directions. There are both actions and reactions, because in each situation there may be cooperation, resistance, or negotiation, resulting in mutual influence and learning. The program may try to influence the applied research community through intermediary institutions or it may work directly with the research community. This typology is provided only as an example. Other organizations would have a different configuration of boundary partners.

Intermediary institution: The institution that represents IDRC in the field (for example, an NGO that is implementing a small-grants program).

Applied research community: The research organizations or individual researchers who are implementing the programming activities in the field. For IDRC, this often implies a government, NGO, or university department that is primarily responsible for the research activities.

Development agents or system gatekeepers: The individuals, groups, or organizations who have the power to promote, block, or otherwise influence how the ultimate beneficiaries are reached and affected. For development research, this group often includes the intended users of the research findings.

Beneficiaries: The individuals or groups for whom, or with whom, the program is ultimately working to help improve their economic, social, political, or environmental well-being.

The program's boundary partners can be listed on Design Worksheet 1 on page 51.

Process

Approximate Time **1 hour**

1. The facilitator asks each person to list on a piece of paper those with whom they think the program needs to work directly to encourage the achievement of the vision. The following questions can be used to guide the process: "Who will be the most important actors with whom you work? On whose actions does the success of the program most depend?" The facilitator or someone from the group reads the vision aloud.

2. Participants read their lists out loud and the facilitator writes the names on a flip chart, eliminating any duplication.

   If the group is having trouble identifying people, organizations, or groups, the facilitator can present the IDRC typology (if it is appropriate) to try to stimulate ideas. The facilitator asks: "Among which actors does the program want to encourage change so that they can contribute to the vision?" Other questions that can guide the process are: "Who are the ultimate beneficiaries? Who can the program influence most directly? Who can help or hinder its work?"

   If the group has only identified one boundary partner, the facilitator asks whether change in that boundary partner needs to be supported by others. It may be that the program is only working directly with one type of person, group, or organization, but the facilitator should verify that they are approaching the change process holistically and have not left anyone out.

3. Sometimes the group will identify long lists of boundary partners. In order to start narrowing down the flip chart list and identifying priorities, the facilitator asks, "Where will you put most of your efforts and resources? Who will you work with directly?" These people, organizations, or groups are highlighted either with a star or by starting another list. If the program will not be working with some actors directly, they should be set aside because they are not boundary partners.

   If the group still has a lot of boundary partners, the facilitator goes over the concept of "boundary partner" with them and asks them to consider whether everyone on the list is a boundary partner or if some actors have a different relationship with the program. The facilitator asks, "Do any of them belong together because you are hoping to see a similar change in them or because they play a similar role?" If so, these are grouped together. The facilitator asks whether the program can realistically expect to influence that quantity of boundary partners or if they need to focus.

If the group wants to better articulate the logic of the influence it wants to have through its boundary partners, it can sketch out its boundary partners' boundary partners. These are the people, organizations, or groups with whom the program's boundary partners are working and whom they are trying to influence to contribute to social change and poverty alleviation. The facilitator asks, "Who are your boundary partners going to influence to contribute to the achievement of the vision?" These individuals, organizations and groups are listed on a flip chart.

4. To concretize the list of people, organizations, and groups that are the program's boundary partners, the facilitator asks the group to do a small profile of each boundary partner. For each type of boundary partner (for example, researchers, policymakers, and others) the facilitator asks: "Who have you been working with that you will continue to work with? Who do you need to start working with?" These peoples' names are listed below the boundary partner. Other information, such as their geographic location and willingness to be involved in the program, can also be discussed and listed at this point if necessary.

FACILITATION TIPS

- The concept of boundary partners is quite specific in Outcome Mapping and it may take the group some time to catch on to the notion of planning, monitoring, and evaluating in relation to the people, organizations, and groups with whom they work directly. This is crucial to the development of the monitoring system, so the facilitator may need to explain the concept quite a few times.

- It can be helpful to point out that the notion of boundary partners is nested. The program's boundary partners have boundary partners of their own. Even if those are the actors whom the program ultimately hopes to reach, it is trying to do that through the people, organizations, and groups with whom it works directly, therefore this is where they should plan for and assess results.

STEP 4
Identify the Outcome Challenge

EXAMPLE OUTCOME CHALLENGE

Outcome Challenge 1: The program intends to see **local communities** that recognize the importance of, and engage in, the planning of resource management activities in partnership with other resource users in their region. These communities have gained the trust of the other members of the partnership and the recognition of government officials so that they can contribute constructively to debates and decision-making processes. They are able to clearly plan and articulate a vision of forest management activities and goals that is relevant to their context and needs. They call upon external technical support and expertise as appropriate. They act as champions for model forest concepts in their communities and motivate others in the partnership to continue their collaborative work.

Once the boundary partners have been identified, an outcome challenge statement is developed for each of them. Outcomes are the effects of the program "being there," with a focus on how actors behave as a result of being reached. An outcome challenge describes how the behaviour, relationships, activities, or actions of an individual, group, or institution will change if the program is extremely successful. Outcome challenges are phrased in a way that emphasises behavioural change. They should be idealistic but realistic. This is done for two reasons: it stresses that development is done by, and for, people; and it illustrates that, although the program can influence the achievement of outcomes, it cannot control them. The program contributes to the change, but ultimate responsibility and power for change rests with the boundary partners themselves.

Outcome challenges are phrased so that they capture how the actor would be behaving and relating to others if the program had achieved its full potential as a facilitator of change. The group is encouraged to think about how it can intentionally contribute to the most profound transformation possible. The "challenge" is for the program to help bring about these changes. Because changes in people, groups, and organizations cannot be understood in isolation from one another, the outcome challenge incorporates multiple changes within a single statement rather than breaking them up into separate statements. A set of progress markers will be identified in Step 5 that outlines the progressive levels of change leading to the achievement of the outcome challenge.

In order to keep the discussion as relevant as possible to the vision and mission, outcome challenges tend not to be quantified (for example, in terms of the percentage increase in boundary partners who have changed) or tied to a specific completion date. This also helps, at both the monitoring and evaluation stages, to avoid simply focusing on indicators that are easier to achieve and measure at the expense of more profound qualitative changes. Outcome challenges should not include information about the strategies or activities that the program intends to employ, but rather should describe the qualities of change in the boundary partners' behaviours. Outcome challenges are usually phrased as "The [*program*] intends to see [*boundary partner*] who [*description of behaviours in the active present tense*]."

> The outcome challenges can be listed on Design Worksheet 1 on page 58.

Process

Approximate Time	30 min.
per boundary partner	

This process works best with relatively small groups (up to 20 people), because it requires that all members of the group go up to the front and write on a flip chart. If there are too many participants, a bottleneck is created at the flip chart and the process can take too much time.

The following process is repeated for each boundary partner.

1. The facilitator asks the group to answer the following question individually: "Ideally, in order to contribute to the vision, how will the boundary partner be behaving or acting differently? What new relationships will have been formed? How will existing ones change?" Each participant writes their answers down on a sheet of paper. It is useful to ask people to reflect on a question themselves for a few minutes before having a group discussion, as it gives them an opportunity to concentrate and come up with more thoughtful answers before they have to share them with others.

2. Flip charts and markers are placed at the front of the room and the participants go up and write down how they would like to see the boundary partner behaving. They do not need to go up one after the other, but should be encouraged to go up together, read what their colleagues are writing down, and talk about the various points. They should not duplicate what their colleagues have written, but should add any new elements that expand on the idea. This encourages them to build on each other's ideas.

3. In plenary, the facilitator then reads over the information on the flip charts and the group discusses whether, cumulatively, the points capture the desired changes in the behaviour, relationships, actions, or activities of the boundary partner. To focus the conversation, the facilitator asks a series of questions: "Is anything missing or factually incorrect? What is your first "gut" reaction to the information? Does anything surprise you about the changes included? Is the set of changes overly ambitious or not sufficiently ambitious? Will the boundary partner be better able to contribute to the development process and the vision if they are behaving and relating with others in these ways?" If the boundary partners are present, the facilitator asks them whether what is being defined makes sense in the "real world."

4. While the group is on a break, the facilitator (alone or with volunteers) organizes the various elements into a single outcome challenge statement that describes the state or qualities of the change in the boundary partner. It can be useful to ask one or two of the participants to help draft the statement.

5. Once the group has reconvened, the facilitator reads the outcome challenge statement and asks the group, "If all these changes occurred, would this boundary partner be well placed to contribute to the vision?" The group should respond favourably that the level of change described in the outcome would make a significant difference and is worth working towards.

6. Once outcome challenges have been developed for all the boundary partners, it is useful to review the logic of the vision, mission, boundary partners, and outcome challenges to make sure that they make sense to the group. In order to do this quickly, the facilitator reads the set of outcome challenges and asks the group: "If all these changes occur, will the program have made the contributions to the vision that it wanted to make? Will it have fulfilled its mission?" There should be spontaneous agreement among the participants that these would be the program's ideal contributions. If someone important was omitted, they should be added to the list of boundary partners and an outcome challenge statement should be developed.

It is also important to make sure that the program being designed fits with the implementing organization. The facilitator asks, "Have the necessary links and connections between the program and your organization's mandate been established?" If the goals of the program and the organization are not compatible, then the group should decide whether that is acceptable, and whether they need to redefine certain elements or get buy-in from someone in the organization.

- Rather than composing each outcome challenge in plenary, the participants can be divided into smaller groups to write the outcome challenge statements, and then come together to review and revise them. If there are enough participants, two groups can write the same outcome challenge statement and they can then be compared in plenary. A lighthearted way to keep the smaller groups limited to their time frame is to set an alarm clock to ring after the time they were given to write the outcome challenge has elapsed (for example, 15 minutes).

- If the program has multiple boundary partners but the primary result to be achieved is to change their relationships with one another (for example, to provide a forum for tobacco control researchers, advocacy NGOs, and health departments to work together on policy development), then it is possible to develop one common outcome challenge and set of progress markers for the whole group. In this case, the outcome challenge would describe the ideal relationship between the partners (for example, considering how the partners are relating to one another and who is doing what in the partnership) and the progress markers would lay out the major milestones in the development of their combined partnerships.

DESIGN WORKSHEET 1: PROGRAM FRAMEWORK

Vision:

Mission:

Boundary Partner 1:	Outcome Challenge 1:
Boundary Partner 2:	Outcome Challenge 2:
Boundary Partner 3:	Outcome Challenge 3:
Boundary Partner 4:	Outcome Challenge 4:

STEP 5
Develop Graduated Progress Markers

EXAMPLE PROGRESS MARKERS

Outcome Challenge: The program intends to see **local communities** that recognize the importance of, and engage in, the planning of resource management activities in partnership with other resource users in their region. These communities have gained the trust of the other members of the partnership and the recognition of government officials so that they can contribute constructively to debates and decision-making processes. They are able to clearly plan and articulate a vision of their forest management activities and goals that is relative to their context and needs. They call upon external technical support and expertise as appropriate. They act as champions for model forest concepts in their communities and motivate others in the partnership to continue their collaborative work.

EXPECT TO SEE LOCAL COMMUNITIES:

1	Participating in regular model forest (MF) partnership meetings
2	Establishing a structure for cooperation in the partnership that ensures that all local interests are represented (mechanics of setting up the structure)
3	Acquiring new skills for involvement in the MF
4	Contributing the minimum human and financial resources necessary to get the MF operational

LIKE TO SEE LOCAL COMMUNITIES:

5	Articulating a vision for the MF that is locally relevant
6	Promoting the MF concept and their experiences with MFs
7	Expanding the partnership to include all the main forest users
8	Calling upon external experts when necessary to provide information or meet technical needs
9	Requesting new opportunities for training and extension
10	Producing and disseminating concrete examples of benefits arising from MF activities
11	Identifying opportunities for collaboration with other institutions and actors
12	Identifying opportunities for, and successfully obtaining, funding from a range of sources

LOVE TO SEE LOCAL COMMUNITIES:

13	Playing a lead role in resource management with view to long- and medium-term benefits
14	Sharing lessons and experiences with other communities nationally and internationally to encourage other MFs
15	Influencing national policy debates and policy formulation on resource use and management

Graduated progress markers are identified for each of the outcome challenges that the program is helping to bring about. They show the complexity of the change process associated with each boundary partner and represent the information that the program can gather in order to monitor achievements toward the desired outcome. For a detailed study of progress, the program can conduct an in-depth evaluation, combining the data from the progress markers with information on their context (gathered using other evaluation tools and methods).

A set of progress markers represents a change model for the boundary partner that illuminates the depth and complexity of change being sought. The progress markers should advance in degree from the minimum one would *expect to see* the boundary partner doing as an early response to the program's basic activities, to what it would *like to see* them doing, to what it would *love to see* them doing if the program were having a profound influence. For instance, progress markers that indicate reactive participation by the boundary partner are relatively easy to achieve and are listed first, under "expect to see"; whereas those that indicate more active learning or engagement are listed second, under "like to see"; and those that are truly transformative are listed third, under "love to see." In this way, the program will be able to trace what has been accomplished, while being reminded of what still needs to be achieved. The "love to see" progress markers should be set sufficiently high to represent profound change. These often come directly from the outcome challenge statement. The program will know it is not setting sufficiently challenging progress markers if the "love to see" markers are frequently met by its boundary partners early in the life of the program. Progress markers are generally framed as follows: "*Who? Is doing what? How?*"

Individually, progress markers can be considered as sample indicators of behavioural change, but their real strength rests in their utility as a set. Cumulatively, they illustrate the complexity and logic of the change process. This is something that no single indicator can accomplish.

Progress markers can also be used to describe how the boundary partner is interacting with its own boundary partners, thereby reflecting the indirect influence of the program. A program selects its boundary partners because of the influence it thinks they can have on development, and the progress markers permit this influence to be tracked.

Progress markers are intended as a way for the program to understand and react to the change process in which the boundary partner is engaged. It is only logical that no successful development program strives to change its partners in ways they do not want. The progress markers need to be mutually agreeable, and worthwhile to both the program and the boundary partner. If there are fundamental differences, these need to be resolved. Inherently, the program only facilitates change by helping to remove constraints and providing access to new information and opportunities for the boundary partners. The progress markers can be negotiated with the boundary partners before, during, or after the design workshop to ensure that they are relevant and appropriate.

Some progress markers may be attached to a date (that is, there may be an expectation that they will be reached by a certain point), but this is not obligatory and should not constrain the program's work. Although time lines are a reality in a development program, they are often externally imposed, may not be intrinsically relevant to the vision, and may even distract from the achievements most relevant to the vision. Reaching the "deadline," or the "target," therefore, should not be a primary focus of the program. The purpose of the program is to foster sustained change in boundary partners, and the purpose of the progress markers is to monitor the achievements that contribute to that outcome.

In Stage Two, Outcome and Performance Monitoring, a monitoring system can be devised for these progress markers, using an Outcome Journal to collect data. In order to manage the amount of data that needs to be collected, the program should limit the number of progress markers it sets for each outcome challenge to no more than

- Four "expect to see" progress markers;
- Eight "like to see" progress markers; and
- Three "love to see" progress markers.

Limiting the number of progress markers in this way also makes it possible to quantify results when monitoring the change process, if this is what the program would like to do. This is discussed in Step 9.

> The progress markers for each outcome challenge can be listed on Design Worksheet 2 on page 59.

Process

Approximate Time	45 min.
per boundary partner	

The following process is followed for each boundary partner to be monitored.

1. To begin setting monitoring and evaluation priorities, the facilitator asks the group whether there are certain boundary partners that are more important, that involve greater risk than others, or whose experience provides more potential for learning. These could be monitored more closely. "More important" can mean that the program plans to focus its resources and effort on that actor in the near future (for example, in the first 18 months of a 36-month program), or that the actor is central to the vision, or that changes in the other boundary partners identified are dependent on that actor changing first. Higher risk actors are those with whom the program has less previous experience or those whose current circumstances may present barriers to the desired behaviour. If the group can identify priority actors on which it would like to focus its monitoring and evaluation activities, then the progress markers and strategy maps can be limited to those actors. Nonetheless, the group should set a time to meet at a later date (for example, when they are planning for the second 18 months of a 36-month program) in order to go through the process for the other boundary partners.

2. The facilitator reads the outcome challenge statement and then asks each member of the group to write down answers to the question, "How can the program know that the boundary partner is moving towards the outcome?" The following questions can help to guide the process: "What milestones will be reached as the boundary partners move towards their intended role in contributing to the vision?" The group should try to think of changes in behaviour, activities, or relationships that would happen early on, as well as those that represent deeper change and take more time. Participants write down one idea per index card.

3. The facilitator posts the index cards on the wall, asking the group to select the cards that represent the minimum the program can expect to see achieved by the boundary partner. What would it like to see achieved? What would it love to see achieved? Any duplication in cards should be eliminated. Complimentary ideas should be joined together onto a single index card. The progress markers should

represent observable change in the behaviour, actions, or relationships of the boundary partner. If the group identifies progress markers that would be difficult to observe, the facilitator asks, "How could you tell if this change happened?" In other words, "What would you see if you visited the boundary partners?"

The group discusses the changes in behaviour that have been outlined and arranges them in the order of the change process from simplest to deepest. Ideally, there should be no more than 15 progress markers in the list; otherwise, there will be too much data to collect. If the group identifies too many progress markers, the facilitator asks the group to identify those that best indicate the boundary partner's engagement and show that change is occurring.

4. Once the group is satisfied with the list, the facilitator reads the outcome challenge statement and the set of progress markers and asks, "Does this represent a logical picture of the complexity of the change process through which the boundary partner would progress when moving towards the outcome? Are any important elements missing?" The group should agree that, although the set of progress markers may not describe every change, it does capture the major milestones.

- If the facilitator does not think that a progress marker has been formulated as a change in behaviour, (s)he asks, "Does this really represent a change in the behaviour, actions, or relationships of the boundary partner?" If not, then it should be rewritten in a more appropriate fashion. Sometimes this has to be repeated a number of times before the group makes the distinction between a behavioral progress marker and a more traditional indicator.

- Some groups become confused about the "expect to see" progress markers because they think of them as the baseline situation — the point at which the program starts working with the boundary partners. Instead, the "expect to see" progress markers represent initial changes in the behaviour, actions, activities, or relationships of the boundary partners — changes that indicate a recognition of, or commitment to, the program's goal. These are the behaviours that require reactive participation by the boundary partners and that should occur if the project itself is operating well.

- In order to be challenging and to encourage the deepest transformation possible, the "love to see" progress markers may extend beyond what one program can achieve within its time frame. If the group expresses concern that they will be viewed as a failure because their boundary partners will not achieve all the "love to see" progress markers, the facilitator reassures them that their success will be assessed based on their ability to encourage the greatest transformation possible in the context in which they and their boundary partners are operating, and this transformation will be clearly situated in the context of the visionary change to which the program is committed. Of course, this also has to be understood and accepted by the program's managers or donors.

- Outputs (directly observable products of the program) are not tracked independently in Outcome Mapping. If the group wants to record outputs using progress markers, then it can include the behaviours of the producers and users of the outputs that it wants to track. For example, an "expect to see" progress marker for research institutions could be "publishing articles on urban agriculture in internationally recognized scientific journals." Through its monitoring, the program could then track the publications as an output by a particular boundary partner. If this was not adequate, other monitoring methods to track outputs would have to be included.

DESIGN WORKSHEET 2: PROGRESS MARKERS

Outcome Challenge:

EXPECT TO SEE _____
[Boundary Partner]

1	
2	
3	
4	

LIKE TO SEE _____
[Boundary Partner]

5	
6	
7	
8	
9	
10	
11	
12	

LOVE TO SEE _____
[Boundary Partner]

13	
14	
15	

STEP 6
Complete a Strategy Map
for Each Outcome Challenge

EXAMPLE STRATEGY MAP		
CAUSAL	**PERSUASIVE**	**SUPPORTIVE**
I-1	**I-2**	**I-3**
▪ fund research projects	▪ run workshops on quantitative and qualitative methods ▪ offer Internet research courses ▪ coordinate training on participatory methods ▪ offer gender sensitivity training to those working with HIV-infected women	▪ hire a professional writer on a retainer to work on dissemination strategies with researchers ▪ hire a fundraiser to help identify donors and develop a fundraiaing strategy ▪ provide ongoing technical assistance
E-1	**E-2**	**E-3**
▪ provide computers and Internet access ▪ include work with women and youth as a condition for the grant	▪ organize regional conferences for HIV/AIDS research community ▪ develop Internet site with tools and methods ▪ publish "special paper" series	▪ establish a formal mentorship program that partners experienced and junior researchers ▪ facilitate the development of an electronic HIV/AIDS policy research network

The purpose of the strategy map is to identify the strategies used by the program to contribute to the achievement of an outcome. A strategy map is created for each outcome challenge. Matrix 1, on page 63, provides a method for dividing strategies into six types. Each of the six cells represents a different type of relationship between the program and the boundary partner it is attempting to influence. For most outcome challenges, a mixed set of strategies will be used because this has a greater potential for success, with one or two being dominant and the remainder being supportive.

Plotting the strategies using this 2 x 3 strategy map will

- Clarify the approach (mix of strategies) used by the program to tackle the particular outcome challenge;
- Indicate the relative influence that the program is likely to have on the individual, group, or organization being targeted;
- Help to pinpoint strategic gaps in the approach or identify whether the program is overextended; and
- Suggest the type of evaluation method appropriate to track and assess the program.

The three strategy types in the first row are labeled "I" because they are aimed directly at specific **individuals**, groups, or organizations. The three strategy types on the bottom row are labeled "E" because they are aimed at the **environment** in which the individuals, groups, or organizations operate. "E" strategies are meant to influence the boundary partners indirectly by altering the setting in which they operate.

Both the "I" and "E" strategy types are further divided into three categories: those that are causal (I-1 and E-1); those relying on persuasion (I-2 and E-2); and those that are based on building supportive networks (I-3 and E-3). Primary control and responsibility for the consequences only rests with the program when I-1 and E-1 strategies are employed. With I-2, I-3, E-2, and E-3 strategies, the program tries to facilitate change, but the ultimate responsibility rests with the individual, group, or institution (i.e., with the boundary partners). The further the program moves away from causal activities, the less control it has. This has important implications for assessing contributions toward the achievement of outcomes.

The purpose of the strategy map exercise is not simply to ensure that all the boxes have something in them. Indeed, some boxes may appropriately be left empty, depending on the nature of the program's work. The appropriateness of strategies largely depends on the type of changes that the program wants to encourage in its boundary partner.

Once the group has completed a strategy map, they can look it over and analyze the total approach. This can help determine whether they are working too much or not enough in certain areas, what relative influence they can expect (given the strategies being employed), and whether they are spreading themselves too thin to have a substantial effect.

In Stage Two, Outcome and Performance Monitoring, a monitoring system can be devised for these strategies, using a strategy journal to collect data.

MATRIX 1: STRATEGY MAP

STRATEGY	CAUSAL	PERSUASIVE	SUPPORTIVE
	I-1	I-2	I-3
Aimed at a Specific Individual or Group	■ Cause a direct effect ■ Produce an output e.g., Deliver money, obtain research, prepare a report	■ Arouse new thinking/skills ■ Always expert-driven ■ Single purpose e.g., Capacity-building activities, skill enhancement, methodological workshops, training	■ Build a support network ■ Based on a supporter/mentor who guides change over time (this could be one person or a group of people) ■ Involvement is more frequent and sustained ■ Nurturing for self-sufficiency ■ Multipurpose (broader intent) e.g., Program member who provides regular guidance and input, expert (management, fundraising...)
	E-1	E-2	E-3
Aimed at Individual's or Group's Environment	■ Change physical or policy environment ■ Incentives, rules, guidelines e.g., Technical transfer, policy change, Internet access, terms of reference (TOR)	■ Disseminate information/ messages to a broad audience ■ Create a persuasive environment ■ Change/alter message system e.g., Radio, TV, Internet, publications, conferences, findings, workshops	■ Create a learning/action network ■ Boundary Partners working together and collectively supporting each other on a regular basis e.g., Research network, participatory research program

The strategy map can be filled out using Design Worksheet 3 on page 67.

Process

Approximate Time per boundary partner	1 hour

This process is followed for each outcome challenge and set of associated progress markers.

1. The facilitator asks each member of the group to write down 7–10 strategies based on the focus question, "How will the program contribute to the achievement of the outcome challenge in the next [appropriate number] months?" These can be new strategies or, if applicable, ones that are already being used.

2. The facilitator then divides the group into pairs so that they can discuss their answers and come up with the five best strategies in which they think the program should engage.

3. Each pair then presents their ideas. The group discusses the strengths and weaknesses of each activity and decides whether it would like to include it in its strategy map. While the group is discussing the various options, the facilitator records the strategies in the correct cell of a strategy map, on a transparency, on a flip chart, or on a computer without showing it to the group. Waiting to show the strategy map until the group has completed the discussion can make it easier to explain the six-cell matrix, because it will be filled with specific examples of the group's work.

4. The facilitator encourages the group to be creative but practical when thinking about strategies. Strategies should not be thought of in isolation. Instead, the group should be encouraged to think about how they complement one another. If the group gets stuck when trying to come up with strategies, the facilitator asks questions such as: "How can you contribute the most with the money you have available in the program? What are the obstacles to the achievement of the outcome? Where and how can you help the boundary partner get around the blockages? What actions can be taken to increase the likelihood of this outcome being achieved? Do you know anybody else who is trying to

contribute to this kind of outcome with this type of boundary partner? Should you act in the same way? Why? Why not? Who else will influence the boundary partner to achieve the outcome and how can you complement their work?"

Before showing the group the strategy map, the facilitator verifies that they have thought through all six strategy types by asking them the following questions about each:

- What will be done to produce an immediate output? [I-1]
- What will be done to build capacity? [I-2]
- How will sustained support, guidance, or mentoring be provided to the boundary partner? By whom? [I-3]
- What will be done to change the physical or policy environment? [E-1]
- How will you use the media or publications to promote your work? [E-2]
- What networks/relationships will be established or used? [E-3]

5. The facilitator presents the completed strategy map to the group and reviews it to make sure that it is complete and realistic, based on the human and financial resources available. The facilitator encourages the group to prioritize by asking, "Are there certain strategies that need to be put in place first? What has to be initiated in the next three or six months? What do you know you have to do, or are already doing and should continue? What is the most promising strategy?" These strategies are highlighted with a star. From amongst those strategies seen as most important, the facilitator asks, "Do you have the necessary resources, capacities, and technical skills to put these strategies into practice?" If not, the group has to decide whether they can compensate for the deficiencies or if they need to devise another strategy.

6. If the group wants to assign specific tasks, a workplan designating staff members' responsibility areas, with a time line for completing tasks, can be developed at this point.

- If the program involves a number of different partners employing strategies to promote the same outcome, the facilitator can use different colours to represent the different partners' strategies on a single map. For example, a coordinating committee's strategies could be listed in red, a research team's strategies in blue, and a peasant organization's strategies in green. This is only appropriate, however, if the combined strategies of the various partners represent the "program" that is using Outcome Mapping.

- The strategy maps are nested, in the sense that a number of different strategies may be required to put one strategy in place. This is particularly true of the I-3 and E-3 strategies. For example, a program attempting to encourage tobacco control advocates to get involved in national health policy development might identify an E-3 strategy of developing a network of policymakers, tobacco activists, health researchers, and evaluators. In order to do this, however, the program would have to offer training to the participants (an I-2 strategy), facilitate an electronic listserv (an E-2 strategy), provide a location for that group to meet (an E-1 strategy), and so on.

DESIGN WORKSHEET 3: STRATEGY MAP

Outcome Challenge:

STRATEGY	CAUSAL	PERSUASIVE	SUPPORTIVE
	I-1	I-2	I-3
Strategies and Activities Aimed at a Specific Individual or Group			
	E-1	E-2	E-3
Strategies and Activities Aimed at Individual's or Group's Environment			

STEP 7
Articulate Organizational Practices

ORGANIZATIONAL
PRACTICES

EXAMPLES OF ORGANIZATIONAL PRACTICES FOR A PROGRAM FOCUSING ON RURAL ENTREPRENEURSHIP	
1. Prospecting for new ideas, opportunities, and resources	The program makes full use of the latest technology and data sources to scan the region and the world for new opportunities to launch or foster new deals.
2. Seeking feedback from key informants	Program staff actively seek the views and opinions of experts in rural entrepreneurship who are working outside the scope of its activities.
3. Obtaining the support of your next highest power	The program engages Board members in the design of its interventions and presents regularly to the Board its progress in identifying, initiating, and closing new deals.
4. Assessing and (re)designing products, services, systems, and procedures	Program staff meet monthly to review experiences of service delivery and systems for identifying and building new deals.
5. Checking up on those already served to add value	Program staff initiate the provision of technical assistance and quality assurance support.
6. Sharing your best wisdom with the world	Program staff identify conferences and workshops on rural entrepreneurship and deliver papers and seminars on the program at least twice each year.
7. Experimenting to remain innovative	The program affords time and space to its staff for reflection on its organizational practices and activities and promotes "outside-the-box" thinking.
8. Engaging in organizational reflection	Program staff meet quarterly to discuss progress in working with their partners to make deals. They conduct annual staff assessments to ensure that adequate human resources are being allotted to programming priorities.

Now that the nature of the work is more clearly defined, the program needs to spend some time looking at how it is going to operate to fulfill its mission. The purpose of this step is to identify the organizational practices that the program will use to be effective. Taken together, these organizational practices describe a well-performing organization that has the potential to sustain change interventions over time.[2] Some of the practices relate directly to the activities being undertaken, whereas others relate to the "care and feeding" of the program so that it can thrive. Collecting and reviewing data on organizational practices contributes in two ways. First, it provides an opportunity to reflect on what is going on internally in the organization, and how that situation could be improved upon so that the program can operate more effectively. In essence, this is about maintaining the relevance of the program, as well as its capacity to stay on top of developments in its field. Second, unintended results often occur in relation to organizational practices, and the opportunity should be taken to document these. For example, through keeping in touch with clients previously served, one may find out about contributions that the program has made outside its intended scope of influence. Unintended results may also occur when making contact with key informants, obtaining the support of the next highest power, and sharing wisdom with others. Unintended outcomes may be important to the survival of a program and may also contribute to new program directions.

In this step, the program reviews the outcome challenges and identifies the organizational practices that will best help it to contribute to the intended change in its boundary partners. In Stage Two, Outcome and Performance Monitoring, a monitoring process can be devised for these practices, using a performance journal to collect data.

EIGHT ORGANIZATIONAL PRACTICES	
1. Prospecting for new ideas, opportunities, and resources	5. Checking up on those already served to add value
2. Seeking feedback from key informants	6. Sharing your best wisdom with the world
3. Obtaining the support of your next highest power	7. Experimenting to remain innovative
4. Assessing and (re)designing products, services, systems, and procedures	8. Engaging in organizational reflection

---

[2] A well-performing organization is defined as one that is efficient, effective, relevant, and sustainable (Lusthaus et al. 1999).

The eight practices are not discrete, nor are they operationalized in a linear fashion. Cumulatively, the practices offer a program a method for considering more broadly the ways in which it works. Each organizational practice represents activities that enable a program to remain relevant, innovative, sustainable, and connected to its environment. The practices are defined below.

Practice 1. Prospecting for new ideas, opportunities, and resources

Members of the program should scan information sources, both locally and globally, for new opportunities that could help them to fulfill their mission. They should be looking for relationships to ongoing activities, as well as entirely new opportunities. These could include new regions in which to work (or that could be linked to existing efforts in other regions) or new groups that could be engaged in the change activity.

Practice 2. Seeking feedback from key informants

In the program's work with its key boundary partners and other organizations that support the delivery of its program (such as other funders), it will likely maintain frequent and regular communication. However, the program should also keep in mind other actors in the field who are not regularly involved, but who have expertise and a robust knowledge of the field of activity. These informants should be people who are willing to be honest and open, and to share both the good and bad impressions made by the program's work with its boundary partners. They can provide feedback that recipients may be unable or unwilling to offer.

Practice 3. Obtaining the support of your next highest power

The program should think about how it is going to present its ideas to higher-level decision bodies in its organization (such as senior management or a board of governors). Good ideas must be presented in an appealing manner that can be understood by decision makers in the context of broader organizational objectives. This involves not only creating opportunities to obtain their support, but also engaging them in activities that strengthen their ownership and commitment to the program. This should be an ongoing process in order to maintain support and interest over time.

Practice 4. Assessing and (re)designing products, services, systems, and procedures

Ongoing review of systems and services is critical to ensuring continued relevance. Once a product or service has been put in place, the program needs to monitor it and to make modifications so that it continues to meet (emerging) needs and demands.

Practice 5. Checking up on those already served to add value

Program staff need to obtain feedback (both positive and negative) from boundary partners. They may find that an earlier project involving the same systems, methods, or products is no longer effective or has created other problems. The program needs to work with its boundary partners to address and fix such problems, and to build the learning from these activities into new work.

Practice 6. Sharing your best wisdom with the world

The program needs to put dissemination procedures in place in order to share its learning. The sharing should be both internal and with external colleagues and networks.

Practice 7. Experimenting to remain innovative

Space needs to be created for a program to explore new directions, tools, and partnerships. This may involve exploring literature not normally associated with the program's work, discussing ideas with those not normally consulted, or taking on challenges beyond its established boundaries. This could include providing informal and individual time for experimentation, organizing group activities, and paying attention to personal and group physical, spiritual, and mental health.

Practice 8. Engaging in organizational reflection

Program members should be viewing each intervention as an opportunity to learn. Efforts should be made to create time for reflection on program performance and direction and on resource allocation.

> The facilitator can capture these actions on Design Worksheet 4 on page 79.

Process
Approximate Time | 30 min.

1. The facilitator presents the concept of organizational practices to the group, highlighting the shift from the subject of boundary partners to the question of how the team will operate to sustain itself and fulfill its mission. The intent in dealing with the organizational practices is to focus on the operating style of the program, making explicit how the group will ensure ongoing creativity and monitoring of its activities, and how it will make itself into a reflective organization. The definitions of the organizational practices can be discussed using examples relevant to the program.

2. The facilitator reviews the outcome challenges with the group in order to identify commonalities. The discussion should focus on how the program will need to operate in order to contribute effectively to these outcome challenges.

3. Taking into consideration the strategies identified in Step 6, the group breaks into pairs to discuss the practices. The facilitator asks them to discuss the following question: "How do you have to be operating in order to support these changes in the boundary partners?" In other words, "What do you have to be doing in terms of the practices in order to remain effective?"

4. Each pair reports back to plenary about the actions associated with the practices in which they think the program needs to engage. The group discusses the benefits and challenges associated with the various practices and actions. Is the practice or action something they currently do? How do they do it? Why is it important? If it is something they do not normally do, why not? The facilitator writes the suggested actions in relation to each of the practices on a flip chart.

5. From the flip chart list, the group identifies the key actions in which they want to engage during the implementation of the program. These key actions can be monitored using the performance journal to be developed in Step 11.

DESIGN WORKSHEET 4: ORGANIZATIONAL PRACTICES

	Key Actions
Practice 1. **Prospecting for new ideas, opportunities, and resources**	
Practice 2. **Seeking feedback from key informants**	
Practice 3. **Obtaining the support of your next highest power**	
Practice 4. **Assessing and (re)designing products, services, systems, and procedures**	
Practice 5. **Checking up on those already served to add value**	
Practice 6. **Sharing your best wisdom with the world**	
Practice 7. **Experimenting to remain innovative**	
Practice 8. **Engaging in organizational reflection**	

4 STAGE 2: OUTCOME & PERFORMANCE MONITORING

INTENTIONAL DESIGN

STEP 1: **Vision**

STEP 2: **Mission**

STEP 3: **Boundary Partners**

STEP 4: **Outcome Challenges**

STEP 5: **Progress Markers**

STEP 6: **Strategy Maps**

STEP 7: **Organizational Practices**

EVALUATION PLANNING

STEP 12: **Evaluation Plan**

OUTCOME & PERFORMANCE MONITORING

STEP 8: **Monitoring Priorities**

STEP 9: **Outcome Journals**

STEP 10: **Strategy Journal**

STEP 11: **Performance Journal**

Introduction to Stage 2

During the Outcome and Performance Monitoring stage of an Outcome Mapping design workshop, the participants can develop a framework to monitor: the progress of boundary partners towards the achievement of outcomes; the program's strategies to support outcomes; and the organizational practices used. First, however, they set monitoring priorities. Based on these priorities, data collection sheets are developed to track outcomes, strategies, and/or organizational practices. An outcome journal (described in Step 9) is suggested for collecting data on the boundary partners' achievement of progress markers. A strategy journal (described in Step 10) is suggested for collecting data on the program's actions in support of the boundary partner. A performance journal (described in Step 11) is suggested for collecting data on the organizational practices being employed by the program to remain relevant, innovative, sustainable, and connected to its environment.

Outcome Mapping helps the program design these data collection instruments, but their value and usefulness will depend on their integration into the program's ongoing management and reporting processes and on the commitment of program members to collect data regularly and reflect on their work honestly. Outcome Mapping cannot interpret the data collected for the program. It is up to the program team to determine what the information means in terms of the program's performance and what needs to be changed, given the team composition; organizational priorities; political, economic, or social contexts; and available resources.

With regular use of these self-assessment tools, the team can reflect upon, and enhance, its performance throughout the implementation of the program. Staff will have the means to ask themselves regularly, "How can we get better at what we are doing so as to increase our contributions to outcomes?" Some of the benefits of regular monitoring meetings will come from the products of those meetings (information gathered that can be used to meet reporting requirements, to feed into evaluations, or to develop promotional materials), while other benefits (such as team building and consensus building) will come from the process of meeting to discuss successes and failures.

Although data is gathered on the program's actions and on changes in its boundary partners, there is no attempt to imply a causal relationship between the two. It is assumed that the program is only one of the many influences on boundary partners. The program can make a logical argument regarding its contributions to changes in its boundary partners, but cannot claim sole credit. By combining the data on external outcomes with data on internal performance, the program will be able to tell learning stories illustrating how it has improved its work in order to encourage the deepest levels of transformation possible in its boundary partners. It can also document the extent to which the partners have moved in the desired directions.

Monitoring Three Parallel Processes

Outcome Mapping recognizes that development is a complex process that is made up of parallel processes. It not only builds an understanding of changes in the development setting in which a program is working, but also monitors and assesses the strategies and activities of a program. Further, it monitors and assesses how a program is operating as an organizational unit. Is the program itself learning and adapting to new conditions and changes in its partners? As such, Outcome Mapping assesses a program holistically and is based on the premise that a program needs to know not only about development results, but also about the processes by which they were attained, as well as about its own internal effectiveness. It is through the combination of information and knowledge in these three areas that a program can build a better understanding of what it is achieving and how it can improve its levels of success.

Through monitoring these three elements of a program — (1) the changes in the behaviors, actions, activities, and relationships of the people, groups, and organizations with whom a program works directly; (2) the strategies that a program employs to encourage change in its partners; and (3) the functioning of a program as an organizational unit — Outcome Mapping unites process and outcome evaluation. Therefore, Outcome Mapping is well suited to the complex functioning and long-term aspects of international development programs where outcomes are intermeshed and cannot be easily or usefully segregated from each other. It provides a program with the information it requires to change along with its partners. Outcome Mapping encourages a program to link itself explicitly to processes of transformation. It focuses on how a program facilitates change rather than on how it causes change, and looks to assess contribution rather than attribution. Looking at how the three elements interrelate and the context in which change occurs is essential to program learning. A program does not operate in isolation of other factors and actors; therefore, it cannot plan and assess as though it does. Systems thinking is not simple, however, as Peter Senge (1990, p. 15) points out:

> Seeing interrelationships, not things, and processes, not snapshots. Most of us have been conditioned throughout our lives to focus on things and to see the world in static images. This leads us to linear explanations of systemic phenomenon.

International development programs are particularly prone to excluding themselves from the system in which development change occurs. By separating themselves from development processes (i.e., something "we" help "them" accomplish) and explaining change using linear reasoning, programs lose the opportunity to explore their full potential as change agents. Outcome Mapping encourages a program to think of itself as part of the change process and to embrace complex reasoning and multiple logic systems (Earl and Carden 2001) .

Will Outcome Mapping Provide the Appropriate Monitoring System?

A sustainable monitoring system must be simple to grasp, be light to implement, provide useful information for learning, and help meet reporting requirements. Monitoring should help the program see its work more holistically. There is no denying that sustaining a monitoring system requires effort and tenacity. Before developing a monitoring system, the group should discuss its readiness to implement the Outcome Mapping monitoring system. Some of the challenges associated with implementing the proposed system are generic to all monitoring systems, while others are specific to Outcome Mapping.

First and foremost is the fact that all monitoring takes time, resources, commitment, and effort. There is no getting around this — it is true of any system selected. If a process is well organized, it should not be difficult; however, it does take work to gather and interpret the data. Outcome

Mapping offers a system to gather data and encourage reflection on

- The progress of external partners towards the achievement of outcomes (What progress markers have been achieved? What evidence demonstrates this change in behaviour, action, or relationship?);
- The internal performance of the program (What mix of strategies are we employing? Are our partners satisfied? How can we improve?); and
- The program's functioning as an organizational unit (How are we doing in helping our partners? Are we learning from experience?).

The program should consider the time and resources it is prepared to spend on the system before embarking on its design. There should be a clear indication from the group about the amount of time and the level of effort that they will realistically be able to put into monitoring. Any system designed should remain within those confines. Monitoring should not be considered in isolation from the other work that the program is doing. Therefore, other reporting and information tracking and sharing activities already being used should be explored, so as to avoid duplication and to link the various monitoring tools to existing processes and practices.

Outcome Mapping encourages the program team to get together, either face-to-face or in an electronic meeting, to collect data and reflect on the program's work. This makes it possible to plan for the future. The frequency of these meetings depends on the group's work schedule, although every two to three months is suggested. If too much time elapses between monitoring sessions, people will forget details and only remember highlights. On the other hand, if meetings are held too frequently, the group may be discouraged by the perceived slowness of change. Each program must establish a monitoring cycle that fits its goals, schedule, and work patterns.

Outcome Mapping was designed primarily as a learning tool for a program that conducts its own monitoring. Although an external monitor can be used to collect data, it is difficult, if not impossible, to contract out learning and appropriate feedback mechanisms. These are not discussed in this manual. One staff member can be assigned to prepare for the meetings and collate the data. Depending on the size and complexity of the program, this should not be an enormous task — it should take approximately one half day per meeting. Having one person responsible will help ensure that the process is not abandoned and that the information from the meetings is recorded and archived systematically. Setting a preassigned day for the meeting helps make it more automatic and routine as well. Once the framework has been established and someone has been assigned the task of gathering information at the meeting, the data can be gathered quite quickly. The group can use the meeting not only to provide data on the recent past, but also to brainstorm ideas and assign tasks for the future. In this way, monitoring becomes an integral part of the program's ongoing management process.

If members of the program cannot meet face-to-face, alternative electronic methods can be developed. For example, each person on the team can fill out the forms separately and submit them by a certain date, and one staff member can be responsible for collation. In this case, however, the final product should be circulated for everyone's information. At some regular interval, however, there should be an opportunity to discuss the information being amassed.

Outcome Mapping is structured around a philosophy of learning and open exchange. The primary purpose of monitoring in Outcome Mapping is to carve out a space where a program can reflect on its experiences in order to feed this knowledge into its planning cycle. A program using Outcome Mapping must be willing to adapt to changing circumstances and learn from its past experiences. If there is not already an environment for sharing experiences and honestly reflecting on performance, Outcome Mapping cannot magically create one. However, it can encourage a more learning-oriented environment by providing a structure for collecting data and for organizing monitoring and evaluation processes.

Outcome Mapping begins from the premise that the easiest and most reliable place to gather data is from those implementing the program. Most of the data collected in the Outcome and Performance Monitoring stage is self-assessment data generated by the program. There are strengths and weaknesses to this approach, and the program should decide whether it is appropriate, given their context and needs, before beginning to design the system. No data is completely objective, whether it is generated internally or externally. Generally, self-assessment data is reliable if it is collected systematically over time. One common concern about self-assessment is that program staff can white-wash failures. Although this is always a possibility, IDRC's experience is that program staff are often more critical of themselves than an external evaluator would be. Furthermore, the self-assessment data collected through monitoring can, if required, be fed into an external evaluation mid-way through the program or after it ends. Regular self-assessment can also help a program to participate more fully in a formal evaluation process by helping the program communicate better with external evaluators.

Self-assessment can also help a program manage its activities better. As C.L. Usher (1995, cited by Fetterman 2001) explains:

> *By developing the capacity to monitor and assess their own performance, program managers and staff can risk the mistakes that often occur with innovation. This is because they can detect problems and make midcourse corrections before the results of errors due to planning or execution become widely apparent and costly. Having the capacity and responsibility to obtain such information about program operations and impact thus empowers managers and staff to explore new ways to enhance their performance.*

Besides those listed above, there are other organizational factors, listed in the table below, that affect the readiness of a program to implement its monitoring system. These should be discussed by the group before it gets into the details of designing a data collection system.

FACTORS THAT CAN AFFECT READINESS TO MONITOR

YOU MUST HAVE:	THESE ARE MIXED BLESSINGS:
■ Acceptance of the monitoring data and system by managers and funders ■ A champion within the program ■ Adequate internal resources (time and people) to do the monitoring ■ A defined use for the monitoring data	■ Other reporting requirements and information tracking and sharing activities ■ Past experience with monitoring (positive or negative)
IT IS NICE TO HAVE:	**THESE CAN BE MAJOR BARRIERS:**
■ Incentives for monitoring and demonstrating learning ■ Additional financial resources to support the monitoring and disseminate the findings	■ Past failures and frustrations with monitoring ■ Superficial or undefined motives ■ Low levels of skill and capability ■ Negative incentives for monitoring

Source: Adapted from Lusthaus et al. (1999).

STEP 8
Setting Monitoring Priorities

Although it is tempting to gather information on a whole range of issues, this is not practical. Monitoring and evaluation priorities need to be set so as not to waste human and financial resources. The first task for the group is to define what they will monitor on an ongoing basis and what they will evaluate in depth in the future. Outcome Mapping identifies three types of information that can be monitored on an ongoing basis, either to demonstrate results or to help improve performance: the organizational practices being employed by the program to remain relevant, innovative, and viable; progress toward the outcomes being achieved by boundary partners; and the strategies that the program is employing to encourage change in its boundary partners. In each element of the monitoring system, the type of information to be gathered is deliberately limited in order to keep the effort manageable and sustainable. Three data collection tools that can be used for monitoring (the outcome journal, strategy journal, and performance journal) are defined in Steps 9, 10, and 11.

The program may choose to implement a "light" monitoring system in which they meet regularly, either face-to-face or electronically, to discuss their boundary partners' achievements and their own strategies or practices. Alternatively, they may choose to implement a "heavier" monitoring system in which they document the data. There are advantages and disadvantages to each approach, and the program needs to determine what works best for its situation.

> The information on the monitoring priorities can be recorded on Monitoring Worksheet 1 on page 86.

Process   **Approximate Time** `1 hour`

Although it is often true that what gets monitored is what gets managed, it is not always possible or useful to monitor everything about a program or its partners. Therefore, the number of boundary partners, or types of strategies, or practices to be looked at should be limited. Outcome Mapping can be modified to consider an entire program broadly, or it can focus on a particular partner or strategy. It is up to the program to determine its priorities.

1. The facilitator describes the three types of monitoring information that Outcome Mapping can help to track: its boundary partners' achievement of progress markers (using an outcome journal); a program's strategy (using a strategy journal); or its organizational practices (using a performance journal). Each of these monitoring tools builds on elements from the Intentional Design stage, so the group should feel relatively comfortable with them.

2. The best way to select monitoring priorities is to think about the uses for the information. Determining in advance how the information will be used allows one to avoid gathering data that, although interesting, has no particular function. To help identify priorities, the facilitator asks the group to consider how the monitoring data collected will be used. Some potential uses for the monitoring data include

   - Improving performance by feeding learning into the management cycle;
   - Helping the program meet reporting requirements;
   - Supplying information for planned evaluations (external or internal);
   - Informing publicity documents and communication activities, or building up case-study materials;
   - Learning about a particular (risky or new) boundary partner, strategy, or practice over time; or
   - Supporting the learning needs of a boundary partner.

   The facilitator asks whether the group wants to monitor strategies, organizational practices, and/or its boundary partners' achievement of progress markers. (S)he asks the group to be as specific as possible about who will use the information; in what documents, presentations, or meetings it will be presented; and when it would be needed in order to be useful.

3. If the group states that it wants to monitor its boundary partners' achievement of progress markers, the facilitator asks the group whether they need to collect data on all their boundary partners or focus their monitoring activities on one or two in particular. In an ideal world, programs would be able to monitor the progress of all their boundary partners, but this is not always feasible, and priorities need to be established. The facilitator tells the group to think realistically about the amount of time it can devote to monitoring and asks, "Which boundary partner do you need to follow most closely (either because it is a new or risky partner, because it will be

your focus over the next little while, because you need to report on your program's contributions to that partner's change process, or for other reasons)?" An outcome journal, to be developed in Step 9, is created for each boundary partner whose achievement of progress markers will be tracked.

4. If the program decides to evaluate a particular strategy in depth, the facilitator identifies where the strategy fits on the strategy map developed in Step 6. Each of the six strategy types implies a different evaluation method. I-1 and E-1 strategies are the most straightforward: quantitative and linear reasoning can be employed because the goal is to check whether the outputs have happened or not. Methods such as cost–benefit analyses or the cataloguing of outputs are appropriate. Monitoring I-2 and E-2 strategies will require more qualitative data, but is still limited to a single event. I-3 and E-3 strategies are the most complex, and data on these strategies can best be captured using story or narrative techniques. A strategy journal, to be developed in Step 10, is created for the selected strategy.

5. When setting monitoring priorities, it is always important to be realistic about what can be managed, given the available human and financial resources. The cost of monitoring depends on how data collection is structured (for example, through group meetings of a team located in the same office, through international workshops, visits, or through teleconferences) and can be as high or low as the program wants. The facilitator confirms with the group that the priorities are realistic by asking, "Who will be responsible for collecting the data? How often will it be collected? What methods are best suited to collecting the data?"

6. Depending on the monitoring priorities established by the program, the facilitator helps the group to develop the content of the monitoring sheets using Steps 9, 10, or 11.

MONITORING WORKSHEET 1: MONITORING PLAN

Monitoring Priority	Who Will Use the Info.?	Purpose of the Info.?	When Is the Info. Needed?	Who Will Collect the Info.?	How Often Will It Be Collected?	How Will It Be Collected?	Proposed Monitoring Tool
Boundary Partner's Achievement of Outcomes							Outcome Journal
Program's Strategy (ies)							Strategy Journal
Program's Organizational Practices							Performance Journal

STEP 9
Develop an Outcome Journal

OUTCOME
JOURNAL

EXAMPLE OUTCOME JOURNAL

Work Dating from/to: Jan.–Mar. 2000

Contributors to Monitoring Update: A. Scott, S. Caicedo, S. Harper

Outcome Challenge: The program intends to see **local communities** that recognize the importance of, and are engaged in, the planning of resource management activities in partnership with other resource users in their region. These communities have gained the trust of the other members of the partnership and the recognition of government officials so that they can contribute constructively to debates and decision-making processes. They are able to clearly plan and articulate a vision of their forest management activities and goals that is relative to their context and needs. They call upon external technical support and expertise as appropriate. They act as champions for model forest concepts in their communities and motivate others in the partnership to continue their collaborative work.

LMH (Low = 0–40%, Medium = 41–80%, High = 81–100%)

	EXPECT TO SEE LOCAL COMMUNITIES	WHO?
OOO	1. Participating in regular model forest (MF) partnership meetings	
●OO	2. Establishing a structure for cooperation in the partnership	Chile
OOO	3. Acquiring new skills for involvement in the MF	
OOO	4. Contributing the minimum human and financial resources necessary to get the MF operational	
	LIKE TO SEE LOCAL COMMUNITIES:	
OOO	5. Articulating a vision for the MF that is locally relevant	
OOO	6. Promoting the MF concept and experiences with MFs	
OOO	7. Expanding the partnership to include all the main actors	
OOO	8. Calling upon external experts when necessary to provide information or meet technical needs	
OOO	9. Requesting new opportunities for training & extension	

OOO	10. Producing and dissemination concrete examples of benefits arising from MF activities	
OOO	11. Identifying opportunities for collaboration with other institutions and actors	
OOO	12. Identifying opportunities for, and successfully obtaining, external funding	

LOVE TO SEE LOCAL COMMUNITIES:

OOO	13. Playing a lead role in resource management with view to long-term benefits	
OOO	14. Sharing lessons and experiences with other communities to encourage other MFs	
OOO	15. Influencing national policy debates and policy formulation on resource use and management	

DESCRIPTION OF CHANGE:

Progress Marker (PM) 2: On June 30, 2000, all MF partners in Chile signed an initiation agreement formalizing a structure and process.

CONTRIBUTING FACTORS AND ACTORS:

The World Wildlife Fund (WWF) held conferences at which the Chile MF was showcased as an example of local partnership. MF members wanted to go to one of these conferences with the formal agreement in place, and did so. The Program Officer provided technical advice on the formulation of agreements based on examples from other MFs worldwide.

SOURCES OF EVIDENCE:

Minutes of Chile MF meetings discussing content of agreement (January 14, June 29, September 14, and December 20, 1999)

Copy of agreement (Jan. 7, 2000) in program file and on MF Web site at <http://www.mf.ch>.

UNANTICIPATED CHANGE:

LESSONS / REQUIRED PROGRAM CHANGES / REACTIONS:

Formal agreements take time to negotiate (one year in this case). To establish ownership and ensure an agreement that reflects the type of partnership wanted by the entire group, a "nurturing" phase is required.

To track progress over time, an outcome journal is established for each boundary partner that the program has identified as a priority. It includes the graduated progress markers set out in Step 5, a description of the level of change as low, medium, or high, and a place to record who among the boundary partners exhibited the change. Information explaining the reasons for the change, the people and circumstances that contributed to the change, evidence of the change, a record of unanticipated change, and lessons for the program is also recorded in order to keep a running track of the context for future analysis or evaluation.

The progress markers are graduated, and some of them, particularly those listed under "like to see" and "love to see," describe a complex behaviour that is difficult to categorize as "having occurred" or "not having occurred." Although many of the progress markers could be the subject of an in-depth evaluation themselves, this is not their intended purpose. The progress markers are not developed as a lockstep description of how the change process must occur; rather, they describe the major milestones that would indicate progress towards the achievement of the outcome challenge. If the program or the boundary partner feel that they are exhibiting the change in behaviour, activities, actions, or relationships described by the progress markers, then that should be noted. At another stage, they may exhibit the achievement of the same progress marker in a different way, and that is perfectly acceptable and should also be recorded. The data collected on the progress markers as a set should reflect the complexity of the change in the people, groups, or organizations, and will invariably need to be contextualized and explained in order to be useful. The purpose of the progress markers in monitoring is to systematize the collection of data on the boundary partners' accomplishments. These details should be viewed as the richness of the results, not as check-marks to be obtained.

The progress markers articulate the results that the program has helped to achieve. They do so by tracking and discussing trends in the behaviours of the boundary partners. Although there is not a cause-and-effect relationship between the program's actions and changes in the boundary partner, by compiling information using the outcome journal, the program will better understand how its actions do, or do not, influence its boundary partners. With this information, the program will be able to improve its own performance and encourage its boundary partners to achieve deeper levels of transformation. The program will also be creating records of observed changes. These records can periodically be synthesized to tell the story of influence and change relative to areas of interest or achievement.

Progress markers should not be viewed as unchangeable during monitoring. If the program does not see changes in its boundary partners over a period of time, then it must ask itself whether the problem is with the progress markers or the strategies being employed to encourage change. Are the progress markers still appropriate (in other words, has the context in which the boundary partner operates changed to the point where the progress markers no longer reflect a desirable or required change)? Does the program need to be doing something else to encourage that change? Has the boundary partner changed direction? If the progress markers are no longer appropriate indicators of change, then they should be revised to reflect the new conditions. In this way, the program will be gathering information on the changing context, and will have information about unexpected results in the boundary partner.

> The outcome journals can be built using Monitoring Worksheet 2 on page 94.

Process

Approximate Time per boundary partner **30 min.**

This process is followed for each boundary partner whose achievements will be monitored over time.

1. The facilitator inserts the outcome challenge and set of progress markers in the outcome journal and then reads them out loud.

2. The facilitator helps the group determine the values for high, medium, and low (HML) ratings so that outcomes can be measured consistently over the course of the program. There can be two different dimensions to the HML ratings:

   - The number of boundary partners exhibiting the change; or
   - The quality or depth of the change exhibited by any one boundary partner.

   If there is a finite number of individuals, groups, or organizations with which the program can work (for example, if 25 organizations comprise one type of boundary partner) then a rating scheme based on percentages is appropriate (for example, where "high" is 80–100%, "medium" is 50–79%, and "low" is 0–49%). If the number of individuals, groups, or organizations is not finite, then the program can set an optimum number that it hopes to work with (for example, five African research institutions over three years). If the program is concerned with the depth of the boundary partner's response, then the values should reflect the quality or consistency of the change (for example, where "high" means that specific actions have been taken in favour of the outcome, "medium" means that the partner is passive or that there is nothing negative to report, and "low" means that actions have been against the behaviour or the goal has been ignored). In each case, the program needs to be able to identify a measurement with which it feels comfortable and which is defensible to anyone looking at the monitoring data.

3. Each boundary partner set can include multiple individuals, groups, or organizations. For example, the program may be working with five women's empowerment NGOs in three countries, but if the changes being sought are the same, they are categorized together, with one outcome challenge statement and one set of progress markers. If this is the case, the facilitator asks the group to identify each boundary partner's starting point in terms of the progress markers. This is necessary if the boundary partners are starting from different stages of development so that their individual change process can be captured over time. For example, if a program works with five research institutions as one boundary partner, where one has already achieved the first two progress markers and the others have not, then that should be noted in the initial outcome journal. This assessment serves as the baseline against which progress is reported over time. The facilitator asks, "Are each of your boundary partners at the same stage (beginning with the first progress marker) or are some of them more advanced than others? Which of your boundary partners are already exhibiting these behaviours?" Sometimes it will not be possible to gather this information on the spot in the meeting, and data will have to be collected and someone assigned to complete the task. If the boundary partners are not present and the group does not feel comfortable making these assessments itself, then the facilitator should help them come up with a process whereby they will include the boundary partners in the process before monitoring begins. This could be done as a self-assessment by the boundary partners.

4. The facilitator reviews each element of the outcome journal and asks the group how their monitoring meetings will proceed.

The facilitator asks, "What method is most appropriate to gather the data?" Some possible options include

- Regular face-to-face meetings where program staff record observed changes in boundary partners based on monitoring visits, documentation, and other evidence;
- Electronic data sheets to be filled out by the program staff on an ongoing basis when changes are noted (these are then aggregated for the entire program);
- Data collected by an external monitor; and
- Interviews or focus groups with boundary partners, the results of which are recorded.

If regular face-to-face or electronic meetings are selected, the facilitator asks: "Who will be responsible for collecting and collating the data? How often will monitoring meetings be held? How can the boundary partners participate in the monitoring process? In what format does the data need to be kept in order to be easily attainable and useful? How can information be constructively fed back to the team and the boundary partners?" The facilitator captures the decisions on a flip chart.

If interviews or focus groups with boundary partners are selected, then the group will need to develop the questionnaires to be used. The group must also answer the following questions: Who will be responsible for organizing, conducting, and collating the data from the focus groups or interviews? How often will the focus groups or interviews be conducted? In what format does the data need to be kept in order to be easily attainable and useful? How can information be fed back to the team and the boundary partners constructively? The facilitator captures the decisions on a flip chart.

5. If desired, the outcome journals can be quantified as a way to facilitate comparison over time (though not as an absolute number for "scoring"). The formula is quite straightforward: the optimum value for any outcome journal is 100. As is the case with any quantitative data, however, it can be interpreted in various ways. Therefore, when it is presented, it should be placed within its context. It is intended to be a tool for monitoring over time. Thus, an absolute value of 21 or 43 is meaningless without knowing previous values. The issue is not the number, but the sequence of numbers and whether progress is being made. In circumstances where numerous boundary partners are being tracked and progress is uneven, this could be a helpful tool to measure overall progress.

Numbers should not be considered absolute; nor should comparisons be made between boundary partners with very different progress markers and starting points. The formula works as follows:

- The high, medium, and low values of the four "expect to see" markers are valued at one point each. (12)
- The high, medium, and low values of the eight "like to see" markers are valued at two points each. (48)
- The high, medium, and low values of the three "love to see" markers are valued at three points each. (27)
- The transition from the "expect to see" to the "like to see" level is valued at five points. (5) (This occurs only when all "expect to see" markers are fulfilled.)
- The transition from the "like to see" to the "love to see" level is valued at eight points. (8) (This occurs when all "like to see" markers are fulfilled.)
- The total possible value, if every marker is fulfilled, is 100.

6. The facilitator discusses work planning with the group and helps them come up with a process that will feed the learning from their monitoring using the outcome journal into their future activities. The planning and management questions they might want to consider during monitoring meetings after completing the outcome journal include the following:

- What are we doing well and what should we continue doing?
- What are we doing "okay" or badly and what can we improve?
- What strategies or practices do we need to add?
- What strategies or practices do we need to give up (those that have produced no results, or require too much effort or too many resources to produce results)?
- Who is responsible? What are the time lines?
- Has any issue come up that we need to evaluate in greater depth? What? When? Why? How?

These questions are listed on Monitoring Worksheet 5 on page 110.

7. At the end of a group activity, it is useful to review what the group has created up to that point. For example, the facilitator asks: "If the program was doing really well and had gathered all this information [read the outcome journal], would that information be illustrative of its work? Is there anything missing? Is this a realistic amount of work, given the resources available?"

MONITORING WORKSHEET 2: OUTCOME JOURNAL

Work Dating from/to:

Contributors to Monitoring Update:

Outcome Challenge:

Low =
Medium=
High=

EXPECT TO SEE			WHO?
LMH			
OOO	1		
OOO	2		
OOO	3		
OOO	4		
LIKE TO SEE			
OOO	5		
OOO	6		
OOO	7		
OOO	8		
OOO	9		
OOO	10		
OOO	11		
OOO	12		
LOVE TO SEE			
OOO	13		
OOO	14		
OOO	15		

MONITORING WORKSHEET 2: OUTCOME JOURNAL

Description of Change:

Contributing Factors & Actors:

Sources of Evidence:

Unanticipated Change:
(include description, contributing factors, sources of evidence)

Lessons / Required Program Changes / Reactions:

STEP 10
Customize a Strategy Journal

Outcome Mapping is based on the premise that the program has to be prepared to change along with its boundary partners. It will need to get better and better at its job in order to respond to its boundary partners' changing needs. In order to provide the program with a systematic way to monitor its actions in support of its boundary partners (so that it can think strategically about its contributions and modify its actions as required), Outcome Mapping provides a monitoring tool called the strategy journal.

The strategy journal records data on the strategies being employed to encourage change in the boundary partners. It is filled out during the program's regular monitoring meetings. Although it can be customized to include specific elements that the program wants to monitor, the generic format includes the resources allocated (inputs), the activities undertaken, a judgement on their effectiveness, the outputs, and any required follow-up.

If gathered regularly and systematically, this information will enable the program to gauge whether it is making optimum contributions to the achievement of outcomes and modify its actions accordingly. To make optimum use of the strategy journal as a learning and management tool, the program, when completing the journal, should not just ask, "How well have we done?" It should also ask, "How can we improve over the next few months?" This dual function is intended to help a program build its own capacity to be effective and relevant.

Together with the information collected in the outcome journal in Step 9 and the performance journal in Step 11, the program will have a systematized set of data about its operations and the results being achieved by its boundary partners. Ideally, the program should be able to make a logical connection between its strategies and its boundary partners' achievement of outcomes — but, again, the relationship is not causal. Analyzing and interpreting the internal and external monitoring data will require the program to reflect on the environment in which it and its partners are operating and contextualize its achievements and failures.

The strategy journal can be built using Monitoring Worksheet 3 on page 101.

Process

| Approximate Time | 1 hour |

Even though there is no information to put into the strategy journal during the design workshop, the facilitator helps the group customize it as required and devise a monitoring process. This will familiarize them with the strategy journal so that they will feel comfortable using it during their monitoring meetings. Some programs may prefer simply to use the strategy journal as a guide for a conversation, while others may want to gather detailed information and evidence. There are no guidelines on which method is better, because it is completely dependent on the needs of the program (in terms of its objectives for the uses of the data). The facilitator asks the group, "How much and what kind of information do you need to collect about your strategies in order to meet your learning needs and reporting requirements?"

The following process is followed for each strategy that the program wants to monitor.

1. The facilitator reviews the various elements of the strategy journal with the group. These include: a description of the activities implemented; a judgement of their effectiveness; a list of the outputs; and a description of the required follow-up and the lessons learned. Over time, the strategy journal is intended to provide the program with information that tells the story of its influence on its boundary partner's development.

2. The facilitator asks the group whether the generic strategy journal contains the necessary information or if there are elements that should be added or deleted. The facilitator asks: "What do you need to be able to document on a regular basis? What would you like to be able to document on a regular basis? What would you like to be able to discuss as a group on a regular basis but do not necessarily need to document?" The strategy journal is customized to the program's needs.

3. If the group has not already gone through the process while designing its outcome journal in Step 9, the facilitator discusses their work planning with them and helps them come up with a process that will feed the learning from their monitoring into their future activ-

ities. The planning and management questions that the group might want to consider during monitoring meetings after completing their strategy journal include the following:

- What are we doing well and what should we continue doing?
- What are we doing "okay" or badly and what can we improve?
- What strategies or practices do we need to add?
- What strategies or practices do we need to give up (those that have produced no results, or require too much effort or too many resources relative to the results obtained)?
- How are/should we be responding to the changes in boundary partners' behaviour?
- Who is responsible? What are the time lines?
- Has any issue come up that we need to evaluate in greater depth? What? When? Why? How?

These questions are listed on Monitoring Worksheet 5 on page 110.

4. If the group has not already gone through the process while designing its outcome journals in Step 9, the facilitator asks how their monitoring meetings will proceed. The facilitator asks what method is most appropriate for gathering the data. Some possible options include:

- Regular face-to-face meetings where program staff record observed changes in boundary partners based on monitoring visits, documentation, and other evidence;
- Electronic data sheets to be filled out by program staff on an ongoing basis when changes are noted (these are then aggregated for the entire program);
- Data collected by an external monitor; and
- Interviews or focus groups with boundary partners, the results of which are recorded.

If regular face-to-face or electronic meetings are selected, the facilitator asks: "Who will be responsible for collecting and collating the data? How often will monitoring meetings be held? How can the boundary partners participate in the monitoring process? In what format does the data need to be kept in order to be easily attainable and useful? How can information be fed back to the team and the boundary partners constructively?" The facilitator captures the answers on a flip chart.

5. At the end of the group activity, it is useful to review what the group has created up to that point. For example, the facilitator asks: "If the program was doing really well and had gathered all this information [read the strategy journal], would that information be illustrative of its work? Is there anything missing? Is this a realistic amount of work, given the resources available?"

Outcome & Performance Monitoring

MONITORING WORKSHEET 3: STRATEGY JOURNAL

Work Dating from/to:	
Contributors to Monitoring Update:	
Strategy to be Monitored:	**Strategy Type:**
Description of Activities (What did you do? With whom? When?)	
Effectiveness (How did it influence change in the boundary partner(s))	
Outputs	
Required Program Follow-up or Changes	
Lessons	
Date of Next Monitoring Meeting:	

STEP 11
Customize a Performance Journal

PERFORMANCE
JOURNAL

Outcome Mapping is based on the premise that the program has to be prepared to change along with its boundary partners. It will need to get better and better at its job in order to respond to its boundary partners' changing needs. In order to provide the program with a systematic way to monitor its actions (so that it can think strategically about its contributions and modify its actions as required), Outcome Mapping provides a monitoring tool called the performance journal.

The performance journal records data on how the program is operating as an organization to fulfill its mission. A single performance journal is created for the program and filled out during the regular monitoring meetings. It includes information on the organizational practices being employed by the program to remain relevant, sustainable, and connected to its environment. Data on these organizational practices can be gathered through quantitative indicators, qualitative examples, or a combination of the two. This learning can then be fed into future work plans.

If gathered regularly and systematically, this information will enable the program to gauge whether it is making optimum contributions to the achievement of outcomes and to modify its actions accordingly. To make maximum use of the performance journal as a learning and management tool, the program, when completing this journal, should not just ask, "How well have we done?" It should also ask, "How can we improve?" This dual function is intended to help a program build its own capacity to be effective.

Together with the information collected in the outcome journal in Step 9 and the strategy journal in Step 10, the program will have a systematized set of data — a map — about its operations and the results being achieved by its boundary partners. Ideally, the program should be able to make a logical connection between its strategies and practices and its boundary partners' achievement of outcomes — but the relationship is not causal. Analyzing and interpreting the internal and external monitoring data will require the program to reflect on the environment in which it and its partners are operating and contextualize its achievements and failures.

> The performance journal can be built using Monitoring Worksheet 4 on page 108.

Process

<table>
<tr><td>**Approximate Time**</td><td>**1 hour**</td></tr>
</table>

Even though there is no information to put into the performance journal during the design workshop, the facilitator helps the group customize it and devise a monitoring process. This will familiarize them with the performance journal so that they will feel comfortable using it themselves during their monitoring meetings. It is also an opportunity to talk abut the actions that can be taken by the team to improve the collective capacity to contribute to change. Some programs may prefer to use the performance journal simply as a guide for a conversation, while others may want to gather detailed information and evidence. There are no guidelines on which method is better, because it is completely dependent on the needs of the program (in terms of its objectives for the monitoring and for the uses of the data). The facilitator asks the group, "How much and what kind of information do you need to collect about your strategies and organizational practices to meet your learning needs and reporting requirements?"

1. The facilitator inserts the key actions for each practice determined in Step 7, and then reviews the various elements of the performance journal with the group. The purpose of the performance journal is to offer a way for the program to reflect and gather data on the actions it is employing to operationalize the practices.

2. The first decision to make is how best to assess and collect information on the practices. The program can qualitatively describe its most significant examples (either positive or negative) over the monitoring period. It can also use quantitative indicators to count the number of times it undertook the key actions for each practice. As an example, a generic set of indicators is provided, below. The facilitator asks the group, "What do you need to be able to document on a regular basis? What would you like to be able to document on a regular basis? What would you like to be able to discuss as a group on a regular basis, but do not necessarily need to document?"

EXAMPLES OF ORGANIZATIONAL PRACTICE INDICATORS

1. **Prospecting for new ideas, opportunities, and resources**

   Number of new ideas shared in the team

   Number of new ideas integrated into the work of the program

2. **Seeking feedback from key informants**

   Number of key informants from whom the program seeks feedback

   Number of changes made to the program because of feedback

3. **Obtaining the support of your next highest power**

   Number of strategic contacts with the next highest power

   Number of hoped for responses from the next highest power

4. **Assessing and (re)designing products, services, systems, and procedures**

   Number of small changes (tweaks) made to existing products, services, systems, and procedures

   Number of significant enhancements to existing products, services, systems, and procedures

5. **Checking up on those already served to add value**

   Number of boundary partners for whom additional services were provided

   Timing/regularity of checking up on those already served

6. **Sharing your best wisdom with the world**

   Number of requests to the program for it to share its "wisdom"

   Number of events/activities where program "wisdom" is shared

7. **Experimenting to remain innovative**

   Number of new ventures into an area without previous experience

   Number of experimental areas that proved successful and were repeated or institutionalized

8. **Engaging in organizational reflection**

   Number and frequency of opportunities for the program team to reflect

   Number of adjustments to the program coming out of a process of organizational reflection

The example used to represent each practice is subjective, but should reflect the action that group members feel has had the greatest effect. A program does not have to do something in each of the eight practice areas in every period, but regularly reviewing all areas may remind the program of an area it is neglecting. The number of key actions should be limited to two or three, otherwise there will be too much data to collect regularly. The facilitator encourages the group to look at both positive and negative examples during their monitoring meetings.

3. If the group did not already do so while developing the outcome journal or strategy journal, the facilitator discusses work planning with them and helps them to come up with a process that will feed the learning from their monitoring into their future activities. The planning and management questions they might want to consider during monitoring meetings after they have completed their performance journal include the following:

- What are we doing well and what should we continue doing?
- What are we doing "okay" or badly and what can we improve?
- What do we need to add to better address the organizational practices?
- What activities do we need to modify (those that have produced no results or require too much effort or too many resources to produce results)?
- Who is responsible? What are the time lines?
- Has any issue come up that we need to evaluate in greater depth? What? When? Why? How?

These questions are listed on Monitoring Worksheet 5 on page 110.

4. If the group did not already go through the process while designing its outcome journal or strategy journal in Steps 9 or 10, the facilitator asks how their monitoring meetings will proceed. The facilitator asks what method is most appropriate to gather the data. Some possible options include

- Regular face-to-face meetings, where program staff record observed changes in boundary partners based on monitoring visits, documentation, and other evidence;
- Electronic data sheets to be filled out by the program staff on an ongoing basis when changes are noted (these are then aggregated for the entire program);

- Data collected by an external monitor; and
- Interviews or focus groups with boundary partners, the results of which are recorded.

If regular face-to-face or electronic meetings are selected, the facilitator asks: "Who will be responsible for collecting and collating the data? How often will monitoring meetings be held? How can the boundary partners participate in the monitoring process? In what format does the data need to be kept in order to be easily attainable and useful? How can information be fed back to the team and the boundary partners constructively?" The facilitator captures the answers on a flip chart.

5. At the end of a group activity, it is useful to review what the group has created up to that point. For example, to sum up the Outcome and Performance Monitoring Stage, the facilitator asks: "If the program was doing really well and had gathered all this information [read the performance journal], would that be illustrative of its work? Would the information be useful? Is there anything missing that would make it really useful? Is this a realistic amount of work, given the resources that are available?"

MONITORING WORKSHEET 4: PERFORMANCE JOURNAL

Work Dating from/to:

Contributors to Monitoring Update:

Practice 1. Prospecting for New Ideas, Opportunities, and Resources

Example or Indicators:

Sources of Evidence:

Lessons:

Practice 2. Seeking Feedback from Key Informants

Example or Indicators:

Sources of Evidence:

Lessons:

Practice 3. Obtaining the Support of Your Next Highest Power

Example or Indicators:

Sources of Evidence:

Lessons:

Practice 4. Assessing and (Re)designing Products, Services, Systems, and Procedures

Example or Indicators:

Sources of Evidence:

Lessons:

MONITORING WORKSHEET 4: PERFORMANCE JOURNAL

Practice 5. Checking Up on those Already Served to Add Value

Example or Indicators:

Sources of Evidence:

Lessons:

Practice 6. Sharing Your Best Wisdom With the World

Example or Indicators:

Sources of Evidence:

Lessons:

Practice 7. Experimenting to Remain Innovative

Example or Indicators:

Sources of Evidence:

Lessons:

Practice 8. Engaging in Organizational Reflection

Example or Indicators:

Sources of Evidence:

Lessons:

Date of Next Monitoring Meeting:

MONITORING WORKSHEET 5: PROGRAM RESPONSE

	Responsible Person	Timing
What should we keep doing?		
What do we need to change in order to improve?		
What strategies/practices do we need to add?		
What strategies/practices do we need to drop (those that have produced no results, or require too much efforts or too many resources to produce results)?		
Has any issue come up that we need to evaluate in greater depth? What? When? Why? How?		

MONITORING WORKSHEET 6: REVIEWING THE LOGIC OF THE PROGRAM

It is important to review the logic of the program periodically to ensure that it remains relevant. Based on practical experience, the program looks at whether new boundary partners have been added; whether others have been dropped; and whether the vision, mission, outcome challenges, and progress markers still make sense. The changes in program logic can then be made to the documentation (for example, Design Worksheet 1 may be revised).

This can be done as often as the program feels is necessary, and can be as heavy or light as the group wishes. It is advisable, however, to incorporate external opinions into the process (such as the views of the boundary partners, experts in the region or in the programming area, managers, donors, and others). The program should also reflect on its monitoring data.

This group activity is not intended to be used in the Outcome Mapping design workshop. This worksheet is intended for the program to use after having collected a substantial amount of data in the journals. The process is as follows:

1. Read the Vision Statement	Does this still reflect the program's dream?
2. Read the Mission Statement	Is this the greatest contribution our program can make? Have we been doing this? Why? Why not? Should we add anything or take anything away?
3. Review Boundary Partners	Is this who we are working with directly? Do we need to work with anyone else?
4. Review Outcomes	Do these accurately describe the ideal way that our boundary partners could act to contribute to the achievement of the vision?
5. Review Progress Markers	Was the change process we set out accurate and useful? What now needs to be added or taken out?
6. Review Strategies	What did we plan to do? Have we implemented these activities? Why? Why not?
7. Review Organizational Practices	Are we doing everything we can to maintain our capacity to support our partners?

5

STAGE 3: EVALUATION PLANNING

INTENTIONAL DESIGN

STEP 1: Vision
STEP 2: Mission
STEP 3: Boundary Partners
STEP 4: Outcome Challenges
STEP 5: Progress Markers
STEP 6: Strategy Maps
STEP 7: Organizational Practices

EVALUATION PLANNING

STEP 12: Evaluation Plan

OUTCOME & PERFORMANCE MONITORING

STEP 8: Monitoring Priorities
STEP 9: Outcome Journals
STEP 10: Strategy Journal
STEP 11: Performance Journal

Introduction to Stage 3

At the Evaluation Planning stage, Outcome Mapping provides a method for the program to identify its evaluation priorities and develop an evaluation plan. The purpose of both monitoring and evaluation is to encourage a program to base its management and programming decisions on systematically collected data rather than on perceptions and assumptions. Using the outcome, strategy, and performance journals for monitoring, the program can gather information that is broad in coverage rather than deep in detail. By conducting an evaluation, the program can choose a strategy, issue, or relationship to study and assess in depth. There will never be sufficient time and resources for a program to evaluate everything, therefore priorities should be set and choices made. Regardless of the evaluation issue selected, however, the program first needs to devise an evaluation plan carefully so that resources are allocated wisely and the evaluation findings are useful. The program needs to be clear about the identification of clients for the in-depth evaluation and ensure their participation in the process. The Evaluation Planning stage offers a process by which a program can do this. The program will not necessary complete the evaluation plan during the Outcome Mapping workshop; it can be developed at any point, whenever the program is preparing to begin an evaluation process.

STEP 12
Develop an Evaluation Plan

The evaluation plan provides a short description of the main elements of the evaluation to be conducted by the program. It outlines the evaluation issue, the way findings will be used, the questions, the information sources, the evaluation methods, the evaluation team, the dates for the evaluation, and the approximate cost. The information in the evaluation plan will guide the evaluation design and, if the program has decided to use an external evaluator, it can be used to set the terms of reference for the contract. Discussing the various elements of the evaluation plan will help the program to plan an evaluation that will provide useful findings. Whether the evaluation is a formal requirement or not, the program should ensure that it is relevant to its needs, in order not to waste human and financial resources.

Even if an evaluation is being done primarily to meet an accountability requirement for an external donor or manager, it can also be used to generate new knowledge, support learning, question assumptions, plan and motivate future activities, or build the analytical capacity of those involved. However, the program needs to plan for utilization, because utilization does not necessarily follow naturally from the results. Michael Quinn Patton argues that, in some ways, assessment is the most straight-forward element of an evaluation, and that the politics of getting findings used is the greatest challenge (Patton 1997).

The information needs of the primary user of the evaluation findings are paramount. The primary user must attend the session when the group is developing the evaluation plan. Getting the client involved in the evalua-tion process from the planning phase will focus data collection activities on the critical issues and prevent the waste of human and financial resources. Regular involvement of the client throughout the phases of data collection and analysis will test the validity of the findings and increase the likelihood of their utilization. Utilization is the ultimate purpose of evaluation, therefore this "front-end" work should be given due attention, whether the program is conducting a self-assessment or responding to external pressure.

EXAMPLE EVALUATION PLAN

Evaluation Issue: Results Achieved by Recipient Research Institutions

Who Will Use the Evaluation? How? When?	Questions	Info. Sources	Evaluation Methods	Who Will Conduct and Manage the Evaluation?	Date (Start & Finish)	Cost
Program management to: 1. Fulfill reporting requirement for donor (due second quarter 2000) 2. Help make sectoral and geographic programming decisions for next phase (planning to begin 05/00) 3. Present findings at donors' forum (in June 2000) 4. Partner institution to use findings to inform program proposal (due 05/00)	What is the profile of the research institutions engaged? How has their capacity to conduct programs changed? What interactions were most/least useful in increasing capacity? Why? What influence has the institution had on research users and other researchers?	Progress Markers & Outcome Journal Trip reports Strategy Journal	Focus groups with research institutions Document review Site visit Key informant interviews with program staff	Senior Consultant with regional and sectoral expertise Managed internally by: A. Gomez A. Beluda	Six months (to be completed by May 1, 2000)	35K

The program will not necessarily complete the evaluation plan during the Outcome Mapping workshop. It can be developed at the point where the program is preparing to begin an evaluation process.

> All the information for the evaluation plan can be captured on Evaluation Worksheet 1 on page 124.

Process   **Approximate Time** | **2 hours**

1. If an evaluation issue was identified earlier, the group reviews whether it is still relevant to their information needs. This can be done by quickly reviewing whether the primary client and purpose of the evaluation have changed and whether formal evaluation findings on the selected evaluation issues and questions are still needed.

2. If the program has not yet identified the evaluation issue it wishes to study in-depth, the facilitator asks a series of questions to encourage the group to discuss the various options and set evaluation priorities. A program cannot evaluate everything, therefore it needs to make strategic choices about what warrants in-depth study. The usual criteria by which a program selects what to evaluate include its learning needs; its accountability or reporting requirements; or its partners' information needs.

   The facilitator asks the group, "What do managers and funders want or need to know about the program? What do we need to report on? What do you currently not know that if you did know would help you be more effective? What information could make a difference to what you do? What areas or issues does the program need to know more about in order to improve? What are your knowledge gaps? What are your partners' knowledge gaps? Is there an issue that you have been monitoring that should be studied in greater depth? What can be done to help the program's partners fulfill their learning and accountability requirements?"

   The group should also consider what it wants to get out of both the evaluation process and the evaluation product. For example, even if the primary purpose of the evaluation findings is to fulfill reporting requirements, the program can plan the evaluation process so that its staff or partners are regularly involved in order to build their evaluation capacity. It is often the learning that takes place in the course of the evaluation process which is most used, rather than the report prepared at the end. This makes the participation of key actors even more important.

3. The facilitator asks the group to identify the individuals, institutions, or agencies that will use the evaluation findings. Although an evaluation report can be disseminated broadly, realistically, it can only be expected to influence its primary audience. The facilitator probes the group for details about how the evaluation findings will be used. The facilitator should try to get the group to be as specific and concrete as possible about who will use the findings and when they will use them. The facilitator asks: "Is there any particular time that the evaluation findings would be most useful? What would encourage or help the user to use the findings?" The group can also discuss how the findings will be used, disseminated or presented to different audiences so as to have maximum impact.

Certain factors are recognized to enhance the likelihood that evaluation findings will be utilized. These include both organizational factors and factors related to the evaluation, as listed below.

ORGANIZATIONAL FACTORS	FACTORS RELATED TO THE EVALUATION
■ Managerial support ■ Promotion of evaluation through a learning culture	■ Participatory approach ■ Timely findings (completion matches organization's planning or review cycle) ■ High quality and relevant data ■ Findings that are consistent with the organizational context ■ Skilled evaluator

Source: El-Husseiny and Earl (1996).

Further elaboration on utilization strategies is provided in Michael Quinn Patton's "Utilization Focussed Flowchart" (Patton 1997, pp. 378–379). The group can also consider dissemination strategies for the intended users of the evaluation findings. The facilitator asks, "How can you most effectively communicate the evaluation findings to the intended users? What format, style, or product would they find most credible as a basis for decisions?"

4. The facilitator asks the group what it is about the issue that they want to know. Each person should have an opportunity to suggest questions. The facilitator writes them on a flip chart and then the group discusses which questions would be the most important and useful to have answered. There are many interesting and important questions that could be asked, but the group needs to prioritize based on their learning needs, their accountability requirements, or their partners' information needs. The questions should be as specific as possible, because vague questions usually yield vague answers.

If multiple suggestions are offered and there is disagreement about which evaluation questions to select, the facilitator provides the group with mock data or answers to each question. The facilitator asks the group, "If you asked question X and received this information back, would it inform your program and help you to improve? What would it change in your program? What would you have to do in response?" (Patton 1997). If, after going through this process, there is still disagreement about which questions to focus on, the facilitator asks if the questions can be sequenced (with some questions answered in this evaluation, and some in another). If at all possible, however, the facilitator should try to avoid compromising the questions to the point where they have all been watered down and nobody's question is answered.

5. The facilitator asks the group what information sources exist that would help to answer the evaluation questions. The use of various information sources permits different perspectives to be incorporated into the evaluation, which increases its credibility. The facilitator asks the group, "Who has the information? What documents would contain that information? What/whose perspectives do these sources cover? Are any missing? Is the information biased?" The Outcome, Strategy, and performance journals can be a valuable source of information for either an internal or an external evaluation.

6. The group brainstorms evaluation methods that would best gather the information needed to answer the evaluation questions. There is no single, perfect evaluation method, but the group should discuss whether each proposed method will provide reliable, credible, and useful findings. Sometimes a less technical evaluation method, as long as it is rigorously applied, is most appropriate, given the time and finances available. Usually a program will use a mix of methods to gather both quantitative and qualitative data. An overview of the most common data-collection methods is offered in Appendix B.

The design and monitoring stages of Outcome Mapping include elements and tools that can be used in an ex-post evaluation to study a strategy, an outcome, the results achieved by a particular boundary partner, or an internal performance issue in greater depth. Much of the data will already have been collected if the program has been using outcome journals, strategy journals, or performance journals for monitoring. If not, the various tools can be adapted for use in a number of ways:

- Even if the program has not used Outcome Mapping from the outset, the elements of the intentional design stage can be used as a first step in an ex-post evaluation to confirm the logic of the program and redefine its vision and mission in outcome terms as the basis for an assessment.
- If the program chooses to do a study of the long-term development impacts that have occurred, the vision, mission, and outcome challenges can be useful. This is because, in developing these ideas, the program was encouraged to describe broad changes that lay beyond the confines of its actions.
- A number of different studies could be crafted around the relationships that did or did not develop with, and among, boundary partners.
- An outcome evaluation could be designed using the progress markers. This could involve collating the monthly monitoring data to track movement and providing a context by explaining the factors that helped and hindered change in the boundary partners; it could also include listing the outputs. If the outcome journals are only being formulated for a summative evaluation, the data may be more difficult to gather, as people tend to forget details and only remember highlights. In this case, the facilitator can ask the group to identify the weaknesses and gaps in the information collected about the boundary partners.[3]
- The eight organizational practices can be used as the criteria for assessing a program's effectiveness. Use of the performance journal to inform an evaluation may also unearth information about the unintended consequences of the program, because the performance journal should provide information about how the program dealt with unexpected issues. These could be studied in greater depth.[4]

---

[3] For an example of an ex-post evaluation using Outcome Mapping, see Armstrong et al. (2000).

[4] For an example of a self-assessment using Outcome Mapping, see NEPED Project (1999).

- The strategy map can be used to review the range of strategies employed by the program in working with its boundary partners. If the program decides to evaluate a particular strategy in depth, it is important to keep in mind that each of the six strategy types implies a different evaluation method. I-1 and E-1 strategies are the most straightforward: quantitative and linear reasoning can be employed because the goal is to check whether the outcomes have happened or not. Methods such as cost–benefit analyses or the cataloguing of outputs are appropriate. An evaluation of I-2 and E-2 strategies will require more qualitative data, but is still limited to a single event. I-3 and E-3 strategies are the most complex, and data on these strategies can best be captured using story or narrative techniques. For a discussion of the story methodology developed by Barry Kibel, see his book, *Success Stories as Hard Data: An Introduction to Results Mapping* (Kibel 1999). For each strategy type, an evaluation could also look at the negative consequences or side-effects, the positive opportunities, and the unexpected results of the program.

When using the strategy maps for an ex-post evaluation, rather than getting the group to identify the entire strategy map, the facilitator can instead query participants only about the dominant strategy employed by the program to promote the achievement of each outcome. The disadvantage of limiting the discussion to the dominant strategy, however, is that the group will not be able to study the full range of their activities in order to identify gaps and better articulate what it is they do.

7. If the evaluation is to be conducted internally, then the name of the staff member conducting the evaluation should be entered into the matrix. If the evaluation is to be conducted by an external consultant, that name should be entered into the matrix; however, the program should still identify an internal person or group of people to be responsible for the evaluation. A collaborative evaluation team will help to ensure that the evaluation remains relevant to the information needs of the program — a key element of the eventual utilization of the findings. The choice of evaluator depends on the type of evaluation to be conducted. As a guideline, however, it is important that an external evaluator understand the purpose of the organization. If the evaluation requires an expert opinion, then a person with a great deal of sectoral expertise and credibility should be sought. If the evaluator will primarily be assessing performance

based on data, then somebody who is familiar with quantitative and qualitative methodologies should be hired.

8. The start and end dates of the evaluation will depend in large part on the type of study to be conducted, however, the group should also consider whether timing is a factor in the utilization of the findings. The facilitator asks, "Could the information to be produced by the evaluation feed into any decision making process? If so, when is that information required?"

9. It is difficult to determine the exact cost of an evaluation before it is designed, but the program should try to estimate the approximate cost and the source of the money. When budgeting for an evaluation, the program should consider the cost of several elements (see Kellogg Foundation 1998):

   - Evaluator fees (per day or lump sum)
   - Travel (transportation and per diems)
   - Workshops (design, findings verification, planning for utilization)
   - Communications (data collection costs, translation)
   - Printing and dissemination
   - Supplies and equipment
   - Use by intended users

10. The facilitator reviews the evaluation plan and asks the group whether the evaluation issue and preliminary design are realistic, based on the levels of human and financial resources, the timeframe, and the types of information available. To test whether the program has developed a strategic evaluation plan, the facilitator reads the plan and asks whether the evaluation data the group is proposing to collect and analyze is worth capturing and, practically, how it will change the work they do. Sometimes it can be a useful exercise to have the group rehearse how they would use the evaluation by providing them with mock findings (positive, negative, and neutral). This can help them to determine whether they are posing the right questions. An exercise in considering the implications of potential findings can also get the group to think through options for improving the program (Patton 1997).

FACILITATION TIP

Even if the group has already gone through the exercise to develop a common understanding of evaluation, it can be very beneficial to repeat this exercise prior to planning an evaluation. This will allow the group to reinforce a common language and make sure that everyone understands the evaluation approach being proposed. This is especially important if any participants have had negative experiences with evaluation in the past or if they will be participating in a new type of evaluation approach (such as participatory evaluation or self-assessment). This exercise is described on page 26.

EVALUATION WORKSHEET 1: EVALUATION PLAN

Evaluation Issue:

Who Will Use the Evaluation? How? When?	Questions	Info. Sources	Evaluation Methods	Who Will Conduct and Manage the Evaluation?	Date (Start & Finish)	Cost

A APPENDIX: Sample Intentional Design Framework

Vision: An expanded global model forest network is gathering support for, creating awareness of, and fostering actions that are consistent with sustainable forest management. In developing, transitioning, and developed countries, local communities, private sector companies, and government officials are partnering together, experimenting with putting the model forest concept into practice, and learning to trust one another. They are redefining their relationships towards each other and towards the natural environment and are influencing national policy debates and policy formulation so that sustainable forests are ensured for future generations. They are expanding their understanding of, and sharing knowledge about, the resource base, and they recognize the interdependence of forest resource values and forest management practices. They are partnering together to negotiate their different perspectives and come up with local solutions that balance conservation needs and desired socioeconomic benefits. Formal and informal decision-making processes involve and benefit all forest users.

Mission: In support of this vision and on behalf of its donors, the program promotes the model forest concept in order to encourage greater participation in setting up and sustaining new model forests and managing existing ones. Its activities at the local and national levels fall into three distinct but interrelated categories: advocacy, coordination, and support. The Secretariat provides opportunities for participants to cooperate and gain greater trust in one another by coordinating and fostering the exchange of information and experience within the network; serving as the channel for the introduction of new ideas and technologies; encouraging experimentation and the use of results of scientific research in improving the performance and output of model forests; and planning and organizing workshops, seminars, and discussions. It helps develop structures for model forest partnerships by providing technical advice and guidance, financial support, and linkages to the Canadian network and other model forest sites. The Secretariat supports the development of the network and champions the concept to international bodies on behalf of its partners.

Boundary Partner 1: Local communities (NGOs, indigenous groups, churches, community leaders, model forest administration unit)	**Outcome Challenge 1:** The program intends to see **local communities** that recognize the importance of, and are engaged in, the planning of resource management activities in partnership with other resource users in their region. They have gained the trust of the other members of the partnership and the recognition of government officials so that they can contribute constructively to debates and decision-making processes. They are able to clearly plan and articulate a vision of their forest management activities and goals that is relative to their context and needs. They call upon external technical support and expertise as appropriate. They act as champions for model forest concepts in their communities and motivate others in the partnership to continue their collaborative work.
Boundary Partner 2: Government officials and policymakers (national forestry agency/department, regional administration)	**Outcome Challenge 2:** The program intends to see **government officials and policymakers** who are committed to the model forest concept and the principles of its partnership. They support the development of local capacity and consult non-traditional groups when planning and making decisions about forest resource management. They are actively involved in the model forest partnership and draw lessons from the experience that are relevant and can be used to inform national policy debates and policy formulation. They champion the model forest concept and seek funding from national and international sources to ensure the continuation and success of the model forest in their country/region.
Boundary Partner 3: Private sector (tourism, fisheries, non-timber forest products, logging and wood processing companies)	**Outcome Challenge 3:** The program intends to see **private sector actors** who are active participants in the model forest partnership and no longer view their goals and forest practices in isolation from other resource users. They recognize that the forest has legitimate multiple resource users and negotiate costs and trade-offs with other, sometimes non-traditional, partners. They encourage economic development while employing sustainable forest practices.

Appendix A

Boundary Partner 4: Academic and research institutions	**Outcome Challenge 4:** The program intends to see **academic and research institutions** that are active members of model forest partnerships and openly share data and tools to assist in decision-making, assessing trade-offs, and understanding environmental impacts at the local level. They see the relevance of the concept on a practical level and are committed to the participatory process for finding local solutions to sustainable forest management.
Boundary Partner 5: International institutions	**Outcome Challenge 5:** The program intends to see **international institutions** that are aware of, and acknowledge, the utility of the model forest concept as a development tool. They integrate it in their planning and programming and advocate the concept to other international donors and international forest bodies. They participate in network activities and other international fora and support efforts to bring in partners at the local and international levels.

B APPENDIX: Overview of Evaluation Methods

METHOD	USE WHEN....
QUESTIONNAIRE SURVEY Involves a printed or electronic list of questions Is distributed to a predetermined group of individuals Individuals complete and return questionnaire	**SURFACE-MAIL OR FAXED SURVEY:** The target population is large (more than 200) You require a large amount of categorical data You require quantitative data and statistical analyses You want to examine the responses of designated subgroups (male/female, for example) The target population is geographically disperse You want to clarify your team's objectives by involving team members in a questionnaire-development exercise You have access to people who can process and analyze this type of data accurately **E-MAIL OR WEB PAGE SURVEY:** You have the appropriate software and knowledge of this method Your respondents have the technological capabilities to receive, read, and return the questionnaire Time is of the essence
FACE-TO-FACE INTERVIEW Involves a printed or electronic list of questions Is distributed to a predetermined group of individuals Individuals complete and return questionnaire	You need to incorporate the views of key people (key-informant interview) The target population is small (less than 50) Your information needs call for depth rather than breadth You have reason to believe that people will not return a questionnaire

METHOD	USE WHEN....
TELEPHONE INTERVIEWS Like a face-to-face interview, but it is conducted over the telephone Interviewer records responses	**ONE-TO-ONE TELEPHONE INTERVIEWS:** The target population is geographically dispersed Telephone interviews are feasible (cost, trust of respondent...) **TELECONFERENCE INTERVIEWS:** The target population is geographically dispersed Equipment is in place
GROUP TECHNIQUE (INTERVIEW, FACILITATED WORKSHOP, FOCUS GROUP) Involves group discussion of predetermined issues or topic Group members share certain common characteristics Facilitator or moderator leads the group Assistant moderator usually records responses Can be conducted in person or through teleconferencing if available	You need rich description to understand client needs Group synergy is necessary to uncover underlying feelings You have access to a skilled facilitator and data has been recorded You want to learn what the stakeholders want through the power of group observation (using a one-way mirror or video)
DOCUMENT REVIEW Involves identification of written or electronic documents containing information or issues to be explored Researchers review documents and identify relevant information Researchers keep track of the information retrieved from documents	The relevant documents exist and are accessible You need a historical perspective on the issue You are not familiar with the organization's history You need hard data on selected aspects of the organization

Boundary Partners	Those individuals, groups, or organizations with whom the program interacts directly and with whom the program can anticipate some opportunities for influence.
Development Impact	Significant and lasting changes in the well-being of large numbers of intended beneficiaries.
Evaluation	A process by which a strategy, issue, or relationship is studied and assessed in-depth.
Evaluation Plan	A short description of the main elements of an evaluation study to be conducted.
Evaluation Planning Stage	The third stage of Outcome Mapping. It helps the program identify evaluation priorities and develop an evaluation plan.
Facilitator	The person who leads a group through the Outcome Mapping design workshop.
Inputs	Resources that are invested into a program in order to encourage results through the relevant activities.
Intentional Design	The planning stage of Outcome Mapping, where a program reaches consensus on the macro level changes it would like to help bring about and plans strategies to provide appropriate support.

Mission	An ideal description of how the program intends to support the achievement of the vision. It states with whom the program will work and the areas in which it will work, but does not list all the activities in which the program will engage.
Monitoring	A process by which data is systematically and regularly collected about a program over time.
Organizational Practices	Eight separate practices by which a program remains relevant, innovative, sustainable, and connected to its environment.
Outcome	Changes in the behaviour, relationships, activities, and/or actions of a boundary partner that can be logically linked to a program (although they are not necessarily directly caused by it).
Outcome Challenge	Description of the ideal changes in the behaviour, relationships, activities, and/or actions of a boundary partner. It is the program's challenge to help bring about the changes.
Outcome & Performance Monitoring Stage	The second stage of Outcome Mapping. It provides a framework for the ongoing monitoring of the program's actions in support of the outcomes and the boundary partners' progress towards the achievement of outcomes. It is based largely on systematized self-assessment.
Outcome Journal	A data collection tool for monitoring the progress of a boundary partner in achieving progress markers over time.

Outputs	Directly achievable and observable, though not necessarily short-term, products of a program.
Performance Journal	A data collection tool for monitoring how well the program is carrying out its organizational practices.
Program	A group of related projects and activities with a specified set of resources (human, capital, and financial) directed to the achivement of a set of common goals within a specified period of time.
Progress Markers	A set of graduated indicators of changed behaviours for a boundary partner that focus on the depth or quality of change.
Reach	Describes how actors were touched by their interaction with the activities and/or results of the research program.
Results	The external effects (outputs, outcomes, reach, and impact) of a program.
Strategy Journal	A data collection tool for monitoring the strategies a program uses to encourage change in the boundary partner.
Strategy Map	A matrix that categorizes six strategy types (causal, persuasive, and supportive), which a program employs to influence its boundary partner. Strategies are aimed at either the boundary partner or the environment in which the boundary partner operates.
Vision	A description of the large-scale development changes (economic, political, social, or environmental) to which the program hopes to contribute.

D APPENDIX: Terms in French, English, and Spanish

FRENCH	ENGLISH	SPANISH
Cartographie des incidences	Outcome Mapping	Mapeo de Alcances
Stade 1. Définition des intentions	**Stage 1. Intentional Design**	**Etapa 1. Diseño intencional**
Étape 1. Vision	Step 1. Vision	Paso 1. Visión
Étape 2. Mission	Step 2. Mission	Paso 2. Misión
Étape 3. Partenaires limitrophes	Step 3. Boundary Partners	Paso 3. Socios directos
Étape 4. Incidences visées	Step 4. Outcome Challenge	Paso 4. Alcances deseados
Étape 5. Marqueurs de progrès	Step 5. Progress Markers	Paso 5. Señales de progreso
Étape 6. Grilles stratégiques	Step 6. Strategy Map	Paso 6. Mapa de estrategias
Étape 7. Pratiques organisationnelles	Step 7. Organizational Practices	Paso 7. Prácticas de la organización
Stade 2. Suivi des incidences et du rendement	**Stage 2. Outcome and Performance Monitoring**	**Etapa 2. Seguimiento de alcances y desempeño**
Étape 8. Priorités du suivi	Step 8. Monitoring Priorities	Paso 8. Prioridades para el seguimiento
Étape 9. Journal des incidences	Step 9. Outcome Journals	Paso 9. Diario de alcances
Étape 10. Journal des stratégies	Step 10. Strategy Journal	Paso 10. Diario de estrategias
Étape 11. Journal du rendement	Step 11. Performance Journal	Paso 11. Diario de desempeño
Stade 3. Planification de l`évaluation	**Stage 3. Evaluation Planning**	**Etapa 3. Planificación de la evaluación**
Étape 12. Plan d'évaluation	Step 12. Evaluation Plan	Paso 12. Plan de evaluación

REFERENCES

Armstrong, J.; Carden, F.; Coe, A.; Earl, S. 2000. IMFNS (International Model Forest Network Secretariat) outcomes assessment. Evaluation Unit, International Development Research Centre. Ottawa, ON, Canada. http://www.idrc.ca/evaluation/finalreport.htm

Earl, S.; Carden, F. 2001. Learning from complexity: IDRC's experience with outcome mapping. Development in Practice (in press).

El-Husseiny, N.; Earl, S. 1996. Enhancing the use of evaluation findings: results of a survey. Evaluation Unit, International Development Research Centre, Ottawa, ON, Canada.

Fetterman, D.M. 2001. Foundations of empowerment evaluation. Sage Publications, Thousands Oaks, CA, USA. pp. 62–63.

ICA (Institute of Cultural Affairs) Canada. n.d. The ToP historical scan. ICA Canada, Toronto, ON, Canada.

Kibel, B.M. 1999. Success stories as hard data: an introduction to results mapping. Kluwer, New York, NY, USA.

Lusthaus, C.; Adrien, M.-H.; Anderson, G.; Carden, F. 1999. Enhancing organizational performance: a toolbox for self-assessment. International Development Research Centre, Ottawa. ON, Canada.

NEPED (Nagaland Environmental Projection and Economic Development) Project. 1999. Nagaland Environmental Projection and Economic Development Project: a self-assessment using outcome mapping. Evaluation Unit, International Development Research Centre, Ottawa, ON, Canada. http://www.idrc.ca/evaluation/nagaland.htm

Patton, M.Q. 1997. Utilization-focused evaluation: the new century text. Sage Publications, Thousand Oaks, CA, USA.

Roche, C. 1999. Impact assessment for development agencies. Oxfam Publishing, Oxford, UK.

Sander, C. 1998. Development research impact: reach. Paper presented at the ICRAF International Workshop on Assessing Impacts in Natural Resource Management Research, 27–29 April 1998, Nairobi, Kenya. Evaluation Unit, International Development Research Centre, Ottawa, ON, Canada. http://www.idrc.ca/evaluation/reach_e.pdf

Senge, P. 1990. The leader's new work: building learning organizations. Sloan Management Review, 32(1), 7–23.

Smutylo, T. 2001. Crouching impact, hidden attribution: overcoming threats to learning in development programs. Draft Learning Methodology Paper prepared for the Block Island Workshop on Across Portfolio Learning, 22–24 May 2001. Evaluation Unit, International Development Research Centre, Ottawa, ON, Canada. http://www.idrc.ca/evaluation/crouching_impact.pdf

Tallmadge, J. 1997. Meeting the tree of life: a teacher's path. University of Utah Press, Utah, USA.

Suchman, E.A. 1967. Evaluative research: principles and practice in public service and social actions programs. Russell Sage Foundation, New York, NY, USA.

Usher, C.L. 1995. Improving evaluability through self-evaluation. Evaluation Practice, 16(1), 59–68.

W.K. Kellogg Foundation. 1998. W.K. Kellogg Foundation evaluation handbook. Kellogg Publications, Battle Creek, MI. USA. http://www.wkkf.org/documents/wkkf/evaluationhandbook/evalhandbook.pdf

THE AUTHORS

Sarah Earl holds a masters degree in Russian politics and development from Carleton University and an MA in Russian history from the University of Toronto. She has carried out research and worked in Eastern Europe and the former Soviet Union, and since 1998 has worked for IDRC's Evaluation Unit.

Fred Carden holds a PhD from the Université de Montréal and a master's degree in environmental studies from York University. He has taught and carried out research at York University, the Cooperative College of Tanzania, the Bandung Institute of Technology (Indonesia), and the University of Indonesia. Dr Carden is coauthor of *Enhancing Organizational Performance* (IDRC 1999) and senior program specialist in IDRC's Evaluation Unit.

Terry Smutylo has been the Director of IDRC's Evaluation Unit since its creation in 1992. He holds a master's degree in African studies from the University of Ghana and an undergraduate degree in sociology from the University of Toronto. Mr Smutylo has worked extensively throughout the developing world and has been involved in conducting evaluations, providing evaluation training, and facilitating workshops in Canada, the United States, Europe, Asia, Africa, and Latin America.

THE PUBLISHER

The International Development Research Centre (IDRC) is a public corporation created by the Parliament of Canada in 1970 to help developing countries use science and knowledge to find practical, long-term solutions to the social, economic, and environmental problems they face. Support is directed toward developing an indigenous research capacity to sustain policies and technologies developing countries need to build healthier, more equitable, and more prosperous societies.

IDRC Books publishes research results and scholarly studies on global and regional issues related to sustainable and equitable development. As a specialist in development literature, IDRC Books contributes to the body of knowledge on these issues to further the cause of global understanding and equity. IDRC publications are sold through its head office in Ottawa, Canada, as well as by IDRC's agents and distributors around the world. The full catalogue is available at http://www.idrc.ca/booktique/.